*Ornamental Trees for
Home Grounds*

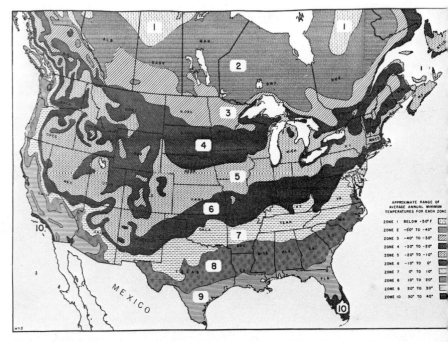

The Zones of Plant Hardiness (*United States Department of Agriculture*, 1960)

Ornamental Trees for Home Grounds

HAROLD O. PERKINS

*Landscape Architect and Professor Emeritus of
Landscape Design, University of Connecticut*

Drawings by Kathleen Bourke

E. P. DUTTON & CO., INC.

NEW YORK

Published simultaneously in Canada by Clarke, Irwin & Company Limited,
Toronto and Vancouver

Contents

PART ONE
Planting and Care

CHAPTER 1

Trees and the Landscape

Plant a tree and you have a bond with tomorrow. One of the nice customs of our forefathers was the planting of a pair of trees—"bride and groom trees"—in front of the new home of a young couple. Some families have followed a practice of planting a young sapling whenever a new member has been added to the family.

We may appear to be less sentimental today, but at least we continue to plant trees about our homes, for we know that trees make a property more livable. They provide natural air conditioning. They temper the sun's rays in the summer and, when properly placed, deflect the cold blasts of winter winds. They absorb sound and give us privacy so that we can more quietly enjoy our own small portion of the world. And they have aesthetic value. Trees soften the severe lines that are so much a part of the man-made world. They give variation to the skyline; they enframe a view; their wonderful assortment of greens soothes the eye and the nerves. The ever-changing and soft shadows may not make a perceptible impact but, even subliminally, they do have an effect on us.

Flowers, shrubs, lawns, trees, supplemented by architectural aids such as fences, walks, terraces, are all part of the well landscaped home. Of these, the trees should be considered of primary importance and planted first since they take a comparatively long period of growth to reach landscape effectiveness.

What's a Tree Worth?

The sentimental value of a tree must be measured personally, but there are monetary values too—not only timber or cordwood values, but those attached to the trees around our homes and bordering our streets.

Fine trees add to the value of a property and thereby affect its resale price. For practical purposes alone, then, there are valid reasons for planting a tree. And with quick depreciation and planned obsolescence the order of the day, it is a relief to find something that actually increases in value as it grows older.

A prominent realtor once said that he could look at the plot of a new subdivision and, without seeing the property itself, could state definitely which lots were blessed with good trees. His system was simple: he merely looked for the first half dozen lots that were marked "Sold," and he could be sure that those were the properties with good trees that would help to make a newly built home more attractive and more livable.

Save a Tree and You Save a Half Century of Waiting

It takes only seconds to cut down a tree that has been fifty years or more in the growing. A shortsighted builder, trying to save a few dollars of grading work by giving the bulldozer operator a free hand, will often denude an area of its trees. He may promise to plant new trees, but he neglects to say how long it will be before they will reach effective landscape size.

The chain saw has been a boon to those concerned with tree removal. But it works with such speed that conservationists, garden club members, and a tree-conscious public must be all the more alert to see that valuable specimens are not lost to the machine.

The advice of a landscape architect as to the location of the house may well mean the saving of fine trees. Several site studies should be made before heavy power equipment is brought in to excavate for basement and foundations. Location of driveways, parking spaces, walks, and paved terraces must be considered in the early planning stages.

Furthermore, three-dimensional thinking is needed. Matters of length and width are not enough; the extra dimension of elevation is most important. Bear in mind that a site plan is just a two-dimensional drawing. It will show, for instance, the location of

An excellent example of what trees add to a community. (*H. Armstrong Roberts*)

the building and driveway on the lot. Any existing trees indicated on such a plan may appear to be safe despite construction development. But if supplementary drawings are prepared, showing the elevation of the building and driveway in relation to existing grades, they may indicate that a considerable change of grade will be necessary. Such a shift of soil level can place a tree in jeopardy by interfering with its roots. Those roots near the earth's surface take in a small but essential amount of oxygen, and if a change of grade results in an extra layer of soil being placed over the root area, the tree can be seriously weakened or

even killed. Conversely, if the grade is lowered to any extent
valuable roots are lost.

A tree that is near the immediate construction area must be
protected by more than a piece of encircling string. The operation
of power equipment requires space in which to maneuver, and
even a glancing blow from a heavy machine may result in serious
damage to living tree tissue. Furthermore, the constant movement
of these machines compacts the soil and thereby reduces the oxygen supply that is required by the tree's surface roots. So sturdy
fencing should be used to insure the safety of the trunk, lower
branches, and roots. Stockpiles of soil designated for future grading should be kept at a safe distance from tree trunks to prevent
the suffocation which can result from burying surface roots for
an extended period. Species vary in their sensitivity to change of
grade, the beech and the hemlock being the most quickly affected.

Justifiable Tree Removal

It simply is not so that a tree is a tree is a tree. Trees are not
all of equal value; some are termed weeds. We pull a weed from
a flower garden to give a desirable plant a better chance to develop; it is even more important to do the same for a tree. After
all, the flower might be affected for one growing season only, but
the tree might receive damage that would be evident for decades
or even a lifetime. Therefore, if your property is overcrowded with
trees, remove the poorer specimens; those remaining will grow
more rapidly and branch better—and will be seen to better advantage.

Why should one tree be considered of greater value than another? Why should some trees be spoken of as weed trees? Because
of their undesirable features. Certain trees have brittle branches
that cannot withstand adverse weather: poplars, willows, silver
maple, and Siberian elm are prime examples. Then, too, the numerous wide-spreading surface roots of these fast-growing trees
clog drain tiles. Hard-to-control borers riddle the trunk of the
black locust. The box-elder with its overabundance of seed

quickly becomes a pest. The fruit of the mulberry stains clothes. Other examples of trees in the weed class could be mentioned. But don't rule out all such trees: what is considered a weed tree under normal conditions may be the best plant available for certain adverse conditions.

There are two sets of values by which a tree is judged: species value and individual value. By species value, we recognize that the oak is more desirable than the poplar because it is longer lived and because it is stronger of limb, hence less likely to be damaged by wind or sleet. Similarly, the hard or sugar maple is considered a better tree than a soft maple such as the silver maple. Then, too, some species are judged as lower in value because they are more prone to attack by serious infestations of insects or diseases; some species have higher value because they are deep rooted and therefore offer less competition to grass or other nearby vegetation. These particulars are brought out in the descriptions of the various trees in Chapter 15.

Individual value takes into consideration physical condition. Are there basal cavities or bad scars on the main trunk? Are there numerous dead branches or undersized, yellowish leaves? These indicate an ailing tree, one that is a poor risk. What is the branching habit? If there is a double leader, two central vertical branches of equal size, structural weakness is indicated. The loss of one of these leaders not only spoils the shape of a tree but also leaves large scars which rarely heal.

There are times, however, when even a good tree must be sacrificed. A house is to be built; space is required not only for the structure but also for the adjacent open areas necessary to provide sunlight and air movement. A road is to be constructed; some distance must be allowed between the path of travel and the tree, both for the safety of the driver and for the survival of a sound tree. According to an old adage, "To make an omelet one must break a few eggs."

If given a choice between saving a desirable tree growing by itself or as part of a cluster, most experts would give preference to the isolated specimen. You see, the group of trees may suffer from the ground-clearing operations: the change in environment may result in weakened trees with numerous dead branches. But the change of exposure to sun and wind, unless exceptional, can act as a stimulant to the "released" tree, which, with competition lessened, will have a chance to develop at an accelerated rate.

Still, if it is possible to protect a cluster, it should be tried. Don't overlook the charm of a clump of trees. The trunk pattern and general growth habit of a group of trees that have existed together for many years offer a natural informality that is difficult for man to duplicate.

New Plantings

The spacing and arranging of trees is a matter for individual case study, but there are some generalities to serve as guides. A minimum spacing of 40 to 60 feet for most trees, with smaller varieties spaced 20 to 30 feet apart, is a safe rule. But great art was never achieved by being slave to "safe rule." In nature we commonly find close plantings, and good designers make use of them to provide a pleasing pattern of verticals near such horizontals as fences, walls, and other structures. A multiple-stemmed tree, which to a timber-minded forester would be a scrub, offers a pleasing line effect. So close planting at times can be most rewarding; it simply requires more thought and more design skill to bring it off effectively.

Shrubs should be grouped together at the edge of your property, not dotted across your lawn. Specimen shrub plantings take up precious space and make the area look small and cluttered. A high-branched tree, even of one of the smaller species, will serve better in such an instance. The unbroken sweep of lawn underneath opens up new vistas and affords a more orderly appearance.

To catch the spirit of nature's plantings takes a discerning eye. Some think that they are making an informal arrangement as long as they use odd-numbered units. All too often three trees will be placed in an equilateral triangle that is mathematically correct to within a fraction of an inch, the trees themselves being equally

Redbud flowers cover both small and large twigs and show the tree's beautiful lines. Here the tree is used to give height and accent to the garden. (*Paul E. Genereux*)

matched in height and trunk caliper. Surely nothing of this sort can be found in nature. Such an arrangement is more artificial than a formally planted allée.

Many a promising lot in a new subdivision is not graced with a tree of any description. If you have bought a treeless plot, you can enhance it by combining the best varieties of large shade trees with small- and medium-sized trees noted for flower, fruit, good foliage, or interesting bark. Place trees 20 feet or more from the house to provide the best setting. When you select a tree with colored bark or flowers, try to achieve informal balance by putting it near a larger tree that is used for shade or framing effectiveness.

While trees are essential, the value of open lawn areas should not be forgotten or ignored. With a background of trees, an unplanted space offers the stimulating contrast of sunlight and shadow. The branches of flowering trees near an open space have a better change to develop and to display their blossoms.

CHAPTER 2

Select, Plant, Maintain

There are many trees available to you, but the final choice for any given set of conditions should be made from a select list— after considerable thought. Remember, trees are not slip covers to be changed as a new season approaches; nor are they automobiles to be turned in for a more recent model. Presumably, you will be living with the tree of your choice for many years.

Whenever new trees are to be added, questions arise. Should a tree be collected or should a nursery-grown plant be purchased? Should the tree be a whip of less than 1-inch caliper; should it be of 2-inch caliper; should it be 6 inches or more in diameter? Is a fast-growing tree desirable, or is a slow-growing species really better? There is no pat answer to any of these questions, but some of the "whys and wherefores" will be considered in the next few paragraphs.

Collected versus Nursery-grown Stock

There just might be a desirable specimen in some out-of-the-way part of your property that you could consider moving. It just might be sufficiently isolated so that its root system has not become entangled with that of another tree. You just might have the time and the muscle to move it at the proper season. And the tree just might live and prosper. You see there are a number of "just might" bridges to cross. It is going to take a greener thumb and a stronger back to move a collected tree successfully than to purchase one from a garden center.

The nursery-grown plant has a number of advantages over one that is collected. It has been root-pruned every few years, which means that in a compact area within a few feet of the trunk you will find a concentration of the important small roots and root hairs which take up water and soluble nutrients. The collected plant, on the other hand, has a widespread root system, and since the smaller roots are at the ends of the larger ones, a high percentage of these essential small roots is lost in the moving process.

It is routine nursery procedure to prune the crown at least once a year and to train the tree to develop a straight trunk and a uniform framework; also, corrective cutting is done to prevent weak structure and to control insects and diseases that might disfigure a plant.

Moreover, the nurseryman offers a wide variety of trees from which to choose. Though native plants may appear in a varied assortment, many are notoriously difficult to transplant. This is particularly true of the tulip tree, pepperidge, white oak, beech, sassafras, walnut, and hickory. More readily transplanted are the maples and elms because of their better root systems. Even then, the nursery-grown tree has the advantage of having been developed under sunlight and air-current conditions far more similar to those of its new planting site than those of the wooded area from which most collected trees come.

WHAT SIZE TO BUY

Since the nursery offers a young tree a better chance for growth than do the home grounds where the lawn competes for its share of soil moisture and nutrients, it is best to buy a tree that is beyond the small whip stage. A tree of 1½- to 2½-inch diameter has the root formation and top growth to ready it for a new spurt once it is transplanted. It is not uncommon for the 2-inch specimen to catch up to, and even surpass, in growth a tree of a size or two larger that has been moved to the same property. The reason is that the smaller plant loses comparatively fewer roots and is more readily handled by the home gardener. So this size may be considered the best buy.

Nevertheless, trees of 6-inch diameter and over are being planted more widely today than in the past. True, they cost considerably more, since it takes several well-trained men with special equipment to move them. The owner is rewarded, however, by having gained trees that are already in scale with his house and by having saved years of waiting for desired shade. In addition, the more finished landscape setting will have increased the value of his property.

Trees of Rapid Growth

Interest in fast-growing trees is quite universal. They appeal to a young family moving into their first home on a plot devoid of trees. They also appeal to older people who have moved to new developments that are complete in everything except trees and who want "some shade in my lifetime."

Some companies not averse to false advertising have taken undue advantage of these desires. Printed claims have been made that certain trees will grow as tall as a house in a year's time. Gullible people send in their money, and before government agencies have time to act, the company has made its profit and moved on.

It is true that there are fast-growing trees, and some species are grown and sold by our better nursery firms. Silver maple, weeping willow, Carolina poplar, Siberian elm, are examples. However, the more we learn about trees, the more we recognize the shortcomings of these plants of rapid growth. They are weak of limb and are therefore readily damaged by a storm. They give a quick return, but they are not trees that future generations will bless us for having planted.

One or two might be planted to give immediate shade, but they should be supplemented by more desirable species and removed as soon as the latter reach a height of 20 to 30 feet. And whenever you plant trees of different growth rates, be sure to set them far enough apart so that the fast-growing ones will not overshadow the more desirable, slower-growing varieties and spoil their shape. When the time comes for cutting down the rapid grower, don't weaken. Let it go, and thus give the better tree a chance.

This subject of the fast-growing tree and consideration of the better species is important. A more complete discussion is to be found in Chapter 11.

The How of Planting

In a sense, the transplanting of a tree is an unnatural process. Nature sows seed to reproduce her kind—she doesn't lift a tree and replant it in a new setting. The best we can do, then, is to lessen the shock of transplanting by recognizing and respecting nature's processes.

A few nurserymen move large trees in winter. To do so requires prior mulching both of the area to be planted and of the ground from which the tree is to be moved so that there will be as little freezing of the soil as possible.

Traditionally, however, transplanting is done in spring and fall when plants are dormant—their growth processes at a low ebb. During this rest period the deciduous tree is without leaves and the evergreen plant exists with but slight transfer of liquids, and so they require only a small amount of water. Add to all this the fact that the ground is not frozen, and you will see why for centuries spring and fall have been the favored seasons for transplanting trees.

One critical factor to be kept in mind is that tree roots are tender and when exposed to dry air, wind, and sunlight, desiccation rapidly takes place. An amateur might unwittingly plant a dead tree—one that died because its roots were left exposed while the planter took a coffee break. To forestall such incidents, nurseries often sell trees which have a ball of soil, held in place with a piece of burlap, around the roots. This is known as the ball and burlap, or B-and-B, method. For many years the B-and-B system was reserved for the more difficult-to-move plants such as magnolia, flowering dogwood, sweet gum, and the evergreens, but it is becoming more commonly used and even the easily moved plants such as maple and crab-apple are now being balled and burlapped instead of sold as bare-root plants.

An even newer development followed by some garden centers is the offering of plants in containers. Plants purchased in this way can easily be removed from the metal or plastic containers and, with soil ball intact, planted at any time the ground is workable.

At the time of planting it is important to supply a good growing mix near the roots; firm the soil to hold the plant in place and to dispel any excess of air near the roots; stake, water, and prune. Following are the pertinent facts.

Planting Procedures

PREPARATION OF PLANTING AREA

Dig a hole of generous proportions, saving the topsoil and discarding the poorer subsoil. If there is any sod keep it separate, being careful to see that it is not placed in contact with or under the roots. (The sod may be broken up and used at the outer perimeter of the hole where it will supply valuable humus as it decomposes.) The hole should be large enough to allow for a 2-inch space below the lower roots and a minimum space of 6 inches beyond the spread of the roots on all sides. Loosen the soil in the bottom of the hole. A mound of soil should be placed under bare-root plants to permit the roots to spread outward as well as downward at an angle.

SOIL MIX

Place a mixture of two-thirds topsoil and one-third peatmoss under and around the tree roots. A moist peat is preferable to the completely dehydrated type. If only the latter is available, place it in a container and saturate it with water before mixing it with the soil.

Fertilizing at time of transplanting is not as important as doing a thorough job of the other steps. Any fertilizing that is done at this time should be slight; use an organic fertilizer that is low in nitrogen. Milorganite or bonemeal may be combined with the soil mix; use six to seven pounds per cubic yard of mix.

PLANTING DEPTH

In general, set a plant at the same depth that prevailed in the nursery. Deep planting, particularly in poorly drained soils, will severely weaken a plant. Beech, flowering dogwood, and evergreens are most sensitive to an excess of soil over their surface roots.

PLANTING

If the plant is a bare-root specimen, spread the roots outward, eliminating any that have a tendency to encircle the trunk. Work the soil between the roots with a small pole or, if the plant is small, shake it gently to induce soil to filter between the roots. If the plant is balled and burlapped, use caution to see that the soil ball is not broken. After the plant has been placed in the hole, loosen the burlap near the top of the ball and roll back the burlap to the sides, but do not remove it. Firm the soil around the plant, using your feet or, for smaller specimens, your hands.

STAKING

Trees that are more than 1 inch in diameter need to be staked to keep them vertical and to prevent swaying which would result in the formation of air pockets near the roots. Larger trees, up to 3-inch diameter, should be supported with a pair of heavy stakes. These should be placed 6 to 10 inches from the tree and should project 3 feet above ground. Near the top of the stake fasten one end of a wire and loop it around the tree. Protect the trunk of the tree from direct contact with the wire. A section of rubber hose over the wire at the point of contact gives the necessary protection. Remove supports after the second year to prevent girdling of the trunk.

The guying of a tree with rope is ineffective. Rope stretches and soon loses its elasticity. Trees of 4-inch or more diameter should be supported with three or more seven-strand wire cables. Use turnbuckles to keep the cables taut at all times. A heavy lag screw should be inserted in the trunk to hold the wire.

WATERING

Water thoroughly at time of planting, using enough to soak the lower roots. Water once a week during the first two years unless there has been a minimum rainfall of an inch during any seven-day period. To make sure that water reaches the lower roots, it is well to use a soaker laid on the ground above the tree roots or a perforated metal rod attached to a hose. The perforated rod, or cane, should be held vertically and plunged into the ground. As the water softens the earth, the rod can easily be worked down 12 or 18 inches to get the water more quickly to root level.

Water is the lifeblood of trees, but when it is given in excess, nature's balance is upset and a plant can be seriously damaged. A small amount of oxygen in the soil is required by the roots. If water displaces this oxygen, the roots become suffocated and fail to function. Plants can be killed by kindness: daily root watering of a newly set plant is an example of such. The tops may be sprinkled daily in early morning or late afternoon, but watering of the roots should be done once or, at the most, twice a week. If watering is done with a hose, it is helpful to have a basin around the tree to hold the water. This may be made by placing a rim of soil at the perimeter of the planting area.

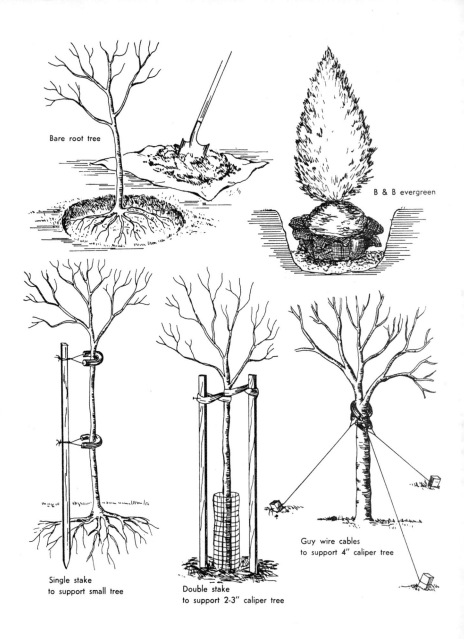

Bare root tree

B & B evergreen

Single stake
to support small tree

Double stake
to support 2-3" caliper tree

Guy wire cables
to support 4" caliper tree

EXTRA PRECAUTIONS

A layer of leafmold, fine wood chips, or other mulch placed on the surface over the root area helps to conserve moisture and prevent the soil from becoming excessively warm. This is desirable during the first two years when numerous new roots are developing.

A newly planted tree 2 inches or more in diameter should have its trunk wrapped to the first major side branches. Use a special tree-wrap paper that comes in rolls 3 inches wide.

Remove all wired labels. These will cause girdling as the tree grows; important branches or even the entire tree may be killed.

EARLY PRUNING

Heavy pruning at time of planting is not now recommended as it was in years past. An adequate supply of leaves is needed to manufacture the food that is returned to the roots. If the tree is to grow, many new roots must be formed; and without sufficient food the growth process will be slow.

Nursery-grown trees with a compact root system require little pruning at time of planting, particularly if they were moved in a ball of soil. But if many roots were lost while transplanting bare-root trees, cut out some of the smaller branches to reduce leaf surface. As much as one-third of the leaf surface can be eliminated without the tree's showing the effect of pruning.

A tree will need some shaping. Cut back some of the longer branches to a small side twig. If crossing branches are in evidence, remove one of them. Look also for the possible development of a double leader. If two branches of equal size are competing to form the central leader, one should be removed, or at least cut back, allowing the other to become dominant. If this is not done, a weak structure will develop and jeopardize the tree's future.

Maintaining

Maintenance doesn't generate the same enthusiasm as planting. When people plant a tree, they visualize it in all its glory. If they think of maintenance at all they place it in the daily toil category. Actually, trees are not demanding in their requirements, but some attention is needed to make a good tree better. If nothing but neglect is proffered the tree's beauty may be spoiled, its life greatly shortened. An economic loss may result for lack of a few pennies' worth of effort. Fertilizing, general care, pest control, pruning, are all part of a maintenance program. Pest control and pruning are discussed in Chapters 3 and 4.

A tree growing under woodland conditions rarely, if ever, needs to be fertilized. Leaves fall, decompose, and return nutrients to the ground. A tree growing on a neatly kept lawn, on the other hand, is in an entirely different situation. The lawn itself lays claim to food and water. Falling leaves must be quickly removed because they will smother the lawn if allowed to remain. "Neatness is starvation," it has been said, and surely this applies to our lawn trees.

Fertilizing Trees

A tree that is in need of emergency feeding displays certain distress signals. Leaves that are smaller than normal and leaves that are yellowish green indicate a lack of soil fertility. The terminal twigs are excessively short, as a result of a slowdown in the rate of growth. Staghead may be evident; that is, the presence of large dead sections near the top of the tree. These are all signs of nutritional weakness, and corrective measures are needed.

Fertilizing a lawn tree calls for special techniques. If the required amount of fertilizer were to be spread on the ground under the tree, it would damage the grass; furthermore, most of it would not penetrate beyond the thick mat of grass roots. Other methods are therefore used.

Under the *punch-hole method,* holes are made approximately a foot deep so that the fertilizer can be placed at tree root level, below the grass root mat. The holes should be 2 to 3 feet apart in a series of concentric rings starting a few feet from the trunk and extending 10 feet or more beyond the spread of the branches. You may work with a power auger or by hand. If you do it by hand, however, you will find it to be a blister-raising affair unless you can wait until the ground is soft, in early spring.

The *water-bar method,* a variation of the punch-hole method, employs a pointed hollow rod which has perforations at the tip and which is attached to a garden hose. It contains a holder for con-

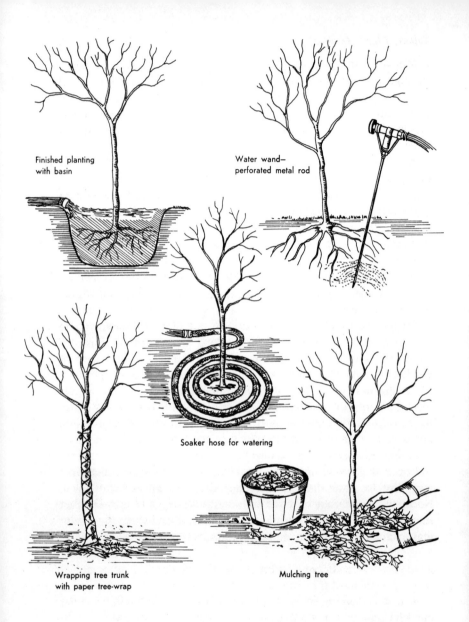

Finished planting
with basin

Water wand—
perforated metal rod

Soaker hose for watering

Wrapping tree trunk
with paper tree-wrap

Mulching tree

centrated fertilizer pellets, which are dissolved as the water passes through the chamber. Since one can't be sure exactly how much nutriment is being supplied by this method, some gardeners use these rods merely as water carriers and as an easy method of making holes in the ground. Dry fertilizer can then be put into the holes.

A 10-6-4 fertilizer, or one with an equivalent formula high in nitrogen, is recommended. Trees that are over 6 inches in trunk diameter (as measured 4½ feet above the ground) should be given three to four pounds of fertilizer for each inch of diameter. Use half this amount for trees that are under 6 inches in diameter. For street trees and others where nearby paved areas reduce the number of feeding holes that can be made, the amount of fertilizer should be reduced by the same proportion as the area which cannot be worked. If a quarter of the area cannot be worked, for instance, use a quarter less fertilizer.

To measure and apply the fertilizer, a metal container such as a small-sized can for frozen orange juice is convenient. Use one canful of fertilizer per hole. The remainder of the hole can be filled with a moist native peat, Michigan peat, or similar product, or composted soil. The entire area should be watered thoroughly to remove any dry fertilizer from the turf; otherwise the lawn will be damaged. Besides, the water places the fertilizer in solution and makes it more readily available to the tree roots.

Spring application of fertilizer is most desirable, and the resulting new growth may be seen within a few weeks. Fertilizer may also be applied in late autumn after the leaves have fallen. No fertilizing should be done between mid-July and mid-October since new growth would not have time to mature before the winter season and would therefore be very subject to frost injury.

What Is Wrong with My Tree?

A tree is lacking in vigor. There is evidently something amiss but what, exactly, is it? The answer might not be immediately obvious even to the trained arborist or tree expert. He might have to do some probing and ask some questions. As we have noted, the tree might be in need of nutriment, or a fill of soil might have weakened it. Then, too, some insect or disease might be responsible. (The problem of pests and diseases is covered in the following chapter.)

There are also several other conditions that might account for the unhealthy appearance. It might be caused by a girdling root, gas injury, chlorosis, or lightning; or a shoot that started from below a graft might have become dominant.

A girdling root is one that partially encircles the tree and cuts into that portion of the trunk which is just below the surface of the ground. Unless it is cut out, it will kill the tree. If detected and removed early enough, the tree, after being fertilized, will regain its vigor. A tree trunk normally flares out at the ground line. If it does not do so it is an indication either of a girdling root or of an excessive fill of soil that has been placed around the tree.

Occasionally an illuminating gas pipeline may leak, causing gas injury. As a result, leaves turn brown and fall off even in midsummer. Utility companies will test for leaks if requested. If damage has not been severe, the soil should be aerated and then saturated with water.

Chlorosis is a yellowing of the foliage due to some imbalance in nutrients, generally a deficiency. An overabundance of water could be the cause, or an inadequate amount of some essential mineral. Sometimes, for chemical reasons, roots are unable to absorb a needed nutrient. For example, pin oaks growing in non-acid soil frequently become chlorotic because iron, although present, is not available to the plant. The remedy is to apply iron chelates, which are in a form the plant can assimilate. For quick relief, this material can be sprayed on the foliage, but it should also be applied to the soil for longer-lasting results.

Lightning may strike a tree, leaving either large scars or surface damage that may be hardly noticeable. A tree that has been struck may die quickly, or a year or two may elapse before it succumbs. Many trees of course withstand the shock. The tree that is most likely to be hit is the tall or the isolated one. Since these frequently are choice trees, you may wish to protect them with lightning rods. This work is best done by a commercial arborist.

Where trees have been grafted, shoots must not be allowed to develop below the graft. A pink dogwood is always grafted onto a white one. If a branch of the white variety should develop below the graft, it would, because of its greater vigor, eventually smother the pink variety.

Change of Grade

In grading about a new home, a fill of soil is usually necessary. As I mentioned in Chapter 1, this may involve some of the existing trees. It is not enough to place a protective wall around the trunk. Although keeping the soil away from the tree trunk will do some good, the real issue is what happens to the upper roots which need the oxygen in the soil in order to function. A fill of soil can reduce or cut off this oxygen supply, causing a slow death.

How much fill can safely be added without adversely affecting a tree? No precise answer can be given. The type of soil used is a contributing factor. A heavy clay soil has small pore space and is easily compacted. A coarse gravel or even a sandy fill permits air flow to take place. Tree species vary. The beech, tulip, and sugar maple are the most sensitive to any change in existing conditions. Around an elm, poplar, or willow, deep fills may not result in damage, especially if part of the root area can be spared. However, where valuable trees are concerned, it is not worthwhile to take a chance. It is better to follow a few simple precautions to assure a flow of air to the root system.

Place a layer of coarse gravel or crushed stone over the entire area extending from the trunk to a point several feet beyond the spread of the branches. Make the layer approximately 18 inches thick if 6 to 10 inches of topsoil are to be placed over the gravel. The gravel layer may be as shallow as 6 inches where only a minor fill is being made. To prevent soil from filtering into the gravel, use a separation layer of straw or fiber glass insulating

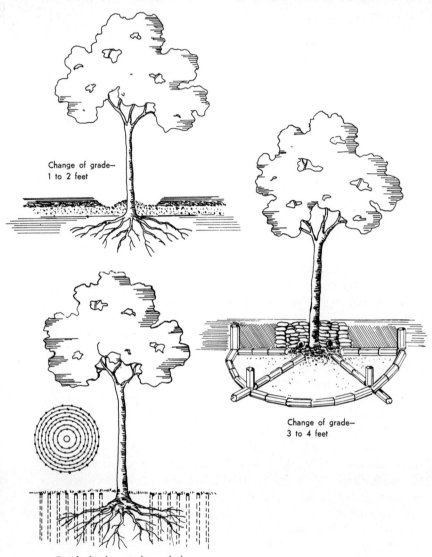

Change of grade—
1 to 2 feet

Change of grade—
3 to 4 feet

Tree feeding by water-bar method

material. You can make the gravel layer near the trunk thicker—to within 2 inches of the surface.

Choice trees that are subject to a fill of 2 feet or more warrant additional attention. Before starting the gravel fill, make a circle of 4- to 6-inch agricultural tile at the drip line; that is, at the outer perimeter of branch spread. Then arrange several radiating lines of tile as a connection to a dry (mortarless) stone wall about the trunk. This wall should be about 2 feet from the tree. The tile should slope downward from the center toward the outer edge so that water will not accumulate near the trunk. Place roofing paper over the tile joints. Then add the 18-inch gravel fill. To prevent the tile inlet from becoming clogged by leaves and other debris, see that the walled-in area near the trunk has a gravel base deep enough to cover the tile.

CHAPTER 3

Pests of Leaf, Stem, and Root

Insects, diseases, and physiological troubles affect plants in a variety of ways. Insect attack is the most readily identified and controlled, because generally the insect itself can be found.

Diagnosis of disease infestations is more difficult and may require microscopic studies or laboratory cultures. The symptoms of disease and of physiological troubles may be similar; or the disease may be secondary, the result of the tree's having been weakened by some physiological irregularity.

Physiological disorders result from poor growing conditions and are indicated by off-color foliage, dead twigs, or stunted growth. They may be classified as the "too, too" troubles. There may be too much water or too much dryness; too much fertilizer or too little. The atmosphere may be poisoned by fumes or the soil by a gas leak or an accumulation of salts from de-icing processes along a road. An improperly mixed spray may damage foliage or the drift of fumes from a weed killer may be harmful.

To Spray or Not to Spray

Sprays can be dangerous, but so can matches. Sprays are generally poisonous; so are many of the household remedies we keep on open shelves in our homes. We need to use care with all of them; so when using spray materials *follow precisely the directions and precautions of the manufacturer.*

Spraying offers the quickest means of combating insect and disease infestation. Not to act quickly might result in a build-up of pests that could do great damage to desirable vegetation. To prevent collateral damage from the sprays themselves, the most lethal ones should be avoided, and spraying should be done from ground level, not from the air, wherever possible.

Sanitation and biological methods are also suggested as pest and disease treatments. Both have their merits and in some instances they offer the best possible solution. For the most part, however, neither singly nor in combination will they suffice to give the desired protection for trees, other ornamental plants, and agricultural crops.

Sanitation calls for the removal of egg masses, the raking and destroying of diseased leaves, the uprooting and burning of infected plants.

Biological control is control by a balance of nature. It is brought about through the use of natural enemies: other insects, animals, or a disease to which an insect is susceptible. Man sometimes tries to introduce a biological control. One of the most recent attempts was through the development of sterile males. Insects are treated with gamma rays in the laboratory and then released. When this practice is followed over a period of several years, a decrease in an insect population or even complete eradication of that insect may result.

A major limitation of the biological control process, however, is the length of time required to try to reach a balance. If there is only one major pest problem to be met, a concentration of scientific effort can be devoted to it and in a few years' time a solution reached. However, the multitude of insect and disease problems cannot all receive attention. If we are to maintain healthy plants or even live plants, we must therefore resort to some use of chemical controls.

Spraying does not always bring the desired results. But this is not always the fault of the spray. Frequently I hear, "I sprayed my tree and it didn't do a bit of good." When I ask what material was used, the answer is all too likely to be, "Oh, something I had on hand. It has worked before on other pests."

Several factors are involved in successful spraying. The proper material is most important: what works on one type of insect will be relatively ineffective against another and worthless against a disease. The exact concentration recommended by the manufacturer must be used. Correct timing is essential. Advice as to the best time to spray in your locality is available from your County Agricultural Agent or State Agricultural Extension Service or Experiment Station. Finally, thorough coverage is necessary. If yours are large trees, you will need an arborist, for he has the heavy equipment needed to obtain a good coverage of the intermediate branches and to reach those at the top.

Specific Pests

LEAF INSECTS—CHEWING

Chewing insects consume all or part of a leaf. Caterpillars, beetles, leaf skeletonizers are found on a variety of trees. Others are more specialized: sawflies on pines and bagworms on junipers. Control measures should start when the insects are first seen. Sevin or DDT can be used for all these pests. Sevin is the safer of the two. DDT has a longer residual effect; that is, it is effective over a longer period so that sprayings need not be as frequent.

Black vine weevils emerge from the soil to eat the edges of rhododendron and yew foliage. Spray such foliage with chlordane to control the mature insects or apply chlordane to the soil in late spring to kill the grubs.

Leaf miners are found on white-barked birches, boxwood, and American holly. Each tree species has its own specific miner. They work between the two leaf tissues, some eating out interior parts of the leaf, others causing structural damage. Malathion or lindane should be used to stop them, since these sprays penetrate the leaf surface; but application must be made early, before the insect has started to make tunnels in the leaf.

LEAF INSECTS—SUCKING

Sucking insects do not damage the outer surface but suck juices from the interior of the leaf. The stomach poisons used for leaf-chewing insects are ineffective. A contact spray should be used: malathion and nicotine sulfate offer effective controls.

Aphids and lace bugs, which attack a variety of plants, also may be controlled by the use of malathion or nicotine sulfate.

Pine needle scale can become numerous enough on mugo pine so that the needles appear to be white. Spray control with malathion should be started *before* such a build-up has taken place.

Gall aphids attack spruce and show up as pineapple-like swellings at the tips of small twigs. They turn brown and look somewhat like a pine cone. Spray with malathion in late winter.

Red-spider mite and honey-locust mite are best controlled with a miticide such as Aramite or Kelthane.

LEAF DISEASES

It is easier to prevent diseases than to control them once they have started. So spraying should be done before the disease has become evident on the foliage. If there has been an infestation one year, there is likely to be an attack the following year unless precautionary steps are taken. Three or four sprayings should be made at weekly intervals unless otherwise indicated.

Leaf blight on hawthorn and leaf spot on mountain-laurel are prevalent in certain areas, especially if there are numerous showers in late spring. Spray hawthorn with lime-sulfur before new spring foliage develops. As the new leaves unfurl, spray with zineb and repeat at two-week intervals. Spray mountain-laurel with zineb or ferbam when the buds break in the spring; repeat at two-week intervals.

Mildew on lilacs does no great harm but it is unsightly. Spray with wettable sulfur or mildex.

Fireblight is a common disease of orchard pears and may be found on related plants. The foliage on isolated branches turns a dark color. Prune out the infested branches, cutting well below the blighted region. Agri-strep and zineb are effective sprays; the first application should be made at blossom time.

Cedar-rust is an alternate-host type of disease. It spends part of its life cycle on the native junipers (including red-cedar) and part on such plants as shadblow and Bechtel crab-apple. Spots made up of concentric rings develop on the foliage of these flowering plants; defoliation takes place in case of a serious attack. Removal of native junipers within a mile radius is one means of control. A spray program combines ferbam and elemental sulfur. Five applications should be made at seven- to ten-day intervals starting in early spring. For best results, spray just before a rainy spell since the fungus spores are most active at that time.

STEM INSECTS

Borers may be found on flowering dogwood, flowering cherry, mountain ash, lilac, and European white birch. DDT sprayed on the trunk or affected branches provides a good control against these insects. The residual effect of this spray is particularly helpful.

Weevils can be very destructive to the terminal twigs of pines. Cut out and burn all infested branches. In the spring, spray pines with a mixture of DDT and malathion; repeat in two weeks.

Hard and soft scales provide a covering for certain sucking insects. Those with a hard covering are found on lilac and fringetree, while the scales on magnolia and yew have a soft covering. For either variety, use a miscible oil as the buds swell in the spring and, if necessary, malathion during the summer.

STEM DISEASES

Cankers may form on branches or trunk of willows and poplars. A break in the bark appears and the area becomes darkened. The wound rarely heals over, and in extreme cases the tree dies within a few years. There is no remedy, but if a tree is kept in vigorous growth it is less susceptible to the disease.

Dutch elm disease is first indicated by a wilting and browning of leaves on isolated branches of the elms. Brown streaks will be found in the sapwood, just under the bark. It may be several years before the tree dies. As yet, there is no effective control, but spraying with DDT or methoxychlor to kill the elm leaf beetle is recommended since this is the insect which spreads the disease. Dead trees should be removed and burned, for they are sources of infection.

Phloem necrosis is an elm disease which is found in the Midwest; so far it has not spread elsewhere. That is fortunate, since it acts even more quickly than Dutch elm disease. It begins at the top of the tree. Leaves curl upward at the margin and are often stiff. Soon the entire tree is affected. There is no known control.

ROOT PESTS

Insects and diseases of the root are hidden from sight and therefore can do considerable damage before their presence is suspected.

The grubs of black vine weevil eat small roots, and in severe cases will girdle the trunk just below the ground surface. They attack rhododendrons and yew. Chlordane is an effective control.

Nematodes are tiny eel-like worms that can be seen only with the aid of a microscope. They attack the roots of boxwood and weaken the plant. Suggested controls are V-C 13 and Nemagon.

CHAPTER 4

Pruning and Cabling

We tend to prune shrubs too much while we neglect to prune our trees. It is true that most trees can go for years without any attention from saw or pruning shears. Nevertheless, there are times when early pruning of a small branch will do much to prolong the useful life of a tree. Much tree pruning can thus be classified as "preventive medicine." A large branch breaks; unless properly pruned, healing of the scar may not take place and wood-rotting fungi will gain a foothold in the trunk, seriously weakening the tree. Double leaders frequently form in certain species; unless reduced to one leader at an early stage, the situation becomes progressively more serious each year.

Pruning

Tree pruning is hazardous business, especially when it is not a short-ladder operation, and so it is best left to a trained commercial arborist or tree surgeon. In some states, arborists are licensed. If licensed arborists or tree experts are not available, a selection should be made from among members of state and national tree-care organizations.

FLUSH CUTS AND TREE PAINT

Where large limbs are to be removed, it is advisable to follow the three-cut system. (1) Using a saw, make an undercut on the limb a foot or two from the trunk; on very large limbs, make the cut even farther from the trunk. Cut as deep as possible, but cease sawing as soon as the weight of the branch binds the saw slightly. If you try to remove the branch with only one cut, the heavy falling limb will strip off a large segment of bark and may make a deep wound that would be unsightly and slow to heal. (2) Several feet beyond the undercut, make a cut from the top of the limb, this time sawing through completely, severing the limb so that only

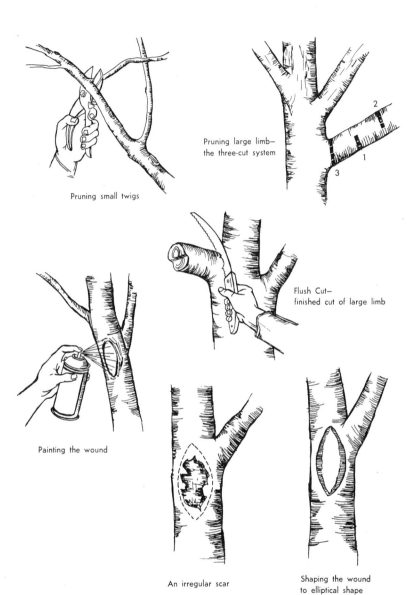

Pruning small twigs

Pruning large limb—
the three-cut system

Flush Cut—
finished cut of large limb

Painting the wound

An irregular scar

Shaping the wound
to elliptical shape

the stub is left. (3) Cut the stub off flush with the trunk, so that callus growth can develop and close over the wound from the sides. No stub, of whatever length, should be allowed to remain: it is unattractive and it cannot possibly heal. It will slowly rot away and, as it does so, wood-rotting fungi will gain a strong foothold in the trunk.

Any wound that is more than an inch or two in diameter should be given a protective coating to keep out fungi. I recommend a special tree paint with a water-emulsified asphalt base. A fresh coating of this black paint should be applied every year until the wound has healed over. Orange shellac may be used as a temporary covering, but it will not be effective for more than a month or so.

The fact that a wound heals from the sides (not from the top or bottom) is too important to be overlooked in any repairs you make. If through some accident a large, irregular piece of bark is removed from the side of a tree, the wounded area should be shaped into a vertical ellipse. This will facilitate the flow of sap and thereby result in more rapid healing from the sides.

Tree pruning can be done at almost any time, although certain seasons are preferable. Late winter is a good time, except for those trees that are known to be bleeders—trees that have a heavy flow of sap, such as the maples and, to a lesser degree, the birches. The sap will exude from the wound. Even though this will not weaken the tree, it disturbs some people; moreover, it will prevent the adherence of tree paint. These trees are best pruned when in leaf: in early summer, preferably, because new growth of wood is starting then and healing will begin quickly.

Cavities—Basal and Upper Trunk

Lawnmowers or cars may hit the base of a tree, causing damage to the bark. If the wound is not treated, a rotted area will develop and spread through the center of the trunk. The tree will live, but it will have lost interior fibers that give it strength to resist high winds and storms.

A tree may be topped either by man or by some act of nature. If a large side branch is lost, and the scar left untreated, rot will enter, and decay will slowly spread throughout the interior. Again, we will have a weak tree.

These injured and untreated trees are potentially dangerous. The crushing power of even one large branch falling from a height of less than 30 feet is greater than most people realize. Action to be taken will depend upon the degree of hazard presented.

If a tree must be removed, the job should be handled by a professional arborist who is fully insured. His insurance is for your protection as well as his own and that of his employees. He takes the tree down limb by limb, using ropes to lower the branches slowly to the ground. He guards against accidents of any kind and uses particular care when working in the vicinity of electrical power lines.

It is commonly thought that if a cavity is present, all that is necessary is to fill it with concrete or some other substance. Actually, when a large cavity exists there is no real advantage in filling it, for no satisfactory repair job can be accomplished when the damage is so great. All unhealthy wood must be removed before any cavity is filled—and the bad wood with its soft rotted fibers extends far beyond what meets the eye. Often it will run the full length of the tree. To remove all of it would weaken the trunk still further, and any cement that might be added would not strengthen the tree a bit.

Tree surgeons do successfully treat and sometimes fill small cavities. Their purpose is to keep water out and to improve the appearance of the tree.

Cabling

Weak structural formation of the larger branches should be watched for and corrected. If two main limbs are competing with each other to become the dominant leader, a tight V-shaped, structurally weak crotch develops. Under the stress of wind or the extra weight of sleet or wet snow, or even under the weight of water on the numerous leaves, an entire side of the tree may be torn away. The falling limb could seriously damage your home, nearby utility lines, passing automobiles, or pedestrians. Even if it did not affect man or property, it would leave a bad scar on the tree, one that might never heal. The tree's symmetry would be ruined and the plant so greatly weakened that there would be little choice but to remove it entirely.

Evidence that a double leader will develop can be detected when two main branches are of no more than pencil-size caliper. At this time, one leader can easily be removed, or at least shortened so that the other will definitely become dominant. But when trees have reached a size where the diameter of the trunk is 6 inches or more, the problem is serious and less easily remedied. The most satisfactory solution at this point is cabling.

Other methods have been tried without success. Iron bands have been placed around the two leaders to hold them together, but as the tree grew over the metal it was weakened further. Heavy metal chains have been used as guys, but rusting took place and when one link gave way all was lost.

A seven-strand braided cable provides a good support. To fasten the cable to the tree, bore a hole through the two branches and insert in each a lag hook, held in place with a nut. The nut should be countersunk to facilitate the bark's growing over it to seal the wound. Don't try to do it yourself: the entire process of cabling is best left to experienced help.

A tree with multiple leaders will require several cables. The bracing will be most effective if these can be placed in a triangular pattern. Cables are normally placed approximately two-thirds of the distance from the crotch to the top of the tree.

CHAPTER 5

Tree Evaluation

Aside from the sentimental value of a tree—a variable for which, as we have noted, there is no top limit—there are monetary factors of which you should be aware.

The price of replacing a large, wide-spreading tree with a near-duplicate could range to fantastic heights, especially if the replacement must be transported any distance over crowded highways and under utility wires and cables. Insurance companies and the Internal Revenue Service are reluctant to accept replacement values that they consider to be excessively high.

If your tree is lost by storm, by accident, or by someone's willful act, you have a case to present. A tree lost through progressive deterioration caused by age will not bring you recompense; neither, at least according to some agencies, will a tree that is lost through insect or disease attack.

As owner, you must *prove* that the value of your property has been lessened. You must set down in dollars and cents exactly what the loss amounts to; you must have the loss appraised by recognized tree and property experts. If you have photographs taken prior to the accident as well as photographs of the damaged tree in relation to the house and other parts of the property, your case is strengthened immeasurably.

There is no absolute scale of prices recognized by appraisers, insurance companies, the Internal Revenue Service—no definite valuation that will stand up in a court of law. But certain standards have been set up which you can use as a guide.

A widely recognized formula was prepared and printed in booklet form some time ago by the International Shade Tree Conference. A revised edition of *Shade Tree Evaluation* was published in 1965. The material that follows is based on this booklet *except that an additional factor, location, has been included.* This appears as "(4) location of tree in relation to buildings and landscape development." I have added this clause because it has such a direct bearing on the extent to which the value of a property is decreased by the loss of a tree.

The several factors used in determining a tree's monetary worth are, then: (1) *size of tree,* (2) *species,* (3) *physical condition,* (4) *location of tree in relation to buildings and landscape development,* (5) *dollar rate per sectional square inch.* The dollar rate has varied over the years as the value of the dollar has changed. In 1957 it was set at $5.00 per square inch of trunk cross section, measured at breast height (4½ feet above ground). The unit price appearing in the 1965 publication of the International Shade Tree Conference is $6.00.

After a tree has been measured and a basic value arrived at, an evaluation is determined by (1) species, (2) physical condition, and (3) location. A tree in perfect physical condition would be rated 100%; others would be scaled at 80%, 60%, 40%, or 20%, depending upon their condition. The same sliding scale applies to location.

When it is an important part of the setting, a large, well-shaped tree such as this White Oak can increase very definitely the monetary value of the property. (*George Taloumis*)

Seven regions have been established by the International Shade Tree Conference with a comprehensive list of trees for each. The regions are New England; Eastern; Southern; Central; Midwestern (including additional lists for Rocky Mountain Irrigated Areas, 4000 to 6000 feet, and Mountain Areas, 6000 to 9000 feet); Western (separate lists for Northern Section—British Columbia; Northern Section—Oregon, Washington; Northern California—Coastal, Inland; Southern California—Coastal, Intermediate, Inner Valley; Nevada, Montana, and Utah); and Canada (separate lists for Ontario and Montreal sections).

To show the relative value of different species, a few typical trees for each of the regions except the Western are given here.

New England

Class 1, 100% — Sugar Maple, White Pine, Red Oak
2, 80% — Norway Maple, London Plane, European Mountain-ash
3, 60% — Horse-chestnut, White Spruce, Weeping Willow
4, 40% — Silver Maple, Tree-of-Heaven, Gray Birch
5, 20% — Box-elder, Catalpa, Pitch Pine

Eastern

Class 1, 100% — Sugar Maple, Flowering Crab-apple, Red Oak
2, 80% — Norway Maple, White Ash, Thornless Honey-locust
3, 60% — Redbud, Chestnut Oak, Austrian Pine
4, 40% — Silver Maple, Norway Spruce, Weeping Willow
5, 20% — Tree-of-Heaven, Catalpa, Carolina Poplar

Southern

Class 1, 100% — Flowering Dogwood, Ginkgo, Southern Magnolia
2, 80% — Pecan, Pepperidge, Carolina Hemlock
3, 60% — Atlas Cedar, Yellow-wood, Sorrel-tree
4, 40% — Water Oak, Green Ash, Shortleaf Pine
5. 20% — Silver Maple, Carolina Poplar, Siberian Elm

Central

Class 1, 100% — Sugar Maple, Red Oak, Little-leaf Linden
2, 80% — Red Maple, European Beech, Pin Oak
3, 60% — Hackberry, Sycamore Maple, Mountain Silverbell
4, 40% — Cutleaf European Birch, Horse-chestnut, White Poplar
5, 20% — Silver Maple, Siberian Elm, Ohio Buckeye

Midwestern

Class 1, 100% — Norway Maple, Sugar Maple, Red Oak
2, 80% — Hackberry, Green Ash, Pin Oak
3, 60% — Black Walnut, Zelkova, Slippery Elm
4, 40% — Horse-chestnut, American Linden, European White Birch
5, 20% — Box-elder, Silver Maple, Catalpa

Canada—Ontario

Class 1, 100% — Norway Maple, Sugar Maple, Little-leaf Linden
2, 80% — European Beech, Pin Oak.
3, 60% — Horse-chestnut, Ginkgo, Cucumber-tree
4, 40% — Catalpa, Kentucky Coffee-tree, Siberian Elm
5, 20% — Box-elder, Tree-of-Heaven, Poplars

Canada—Montreal

Class 1, 100% — Norway Maple, Sugar Maple, Red Oak
2, 80% — Washington Hawthorn, Ginkgo, Thornless Honey-locust
3, 60% — Yellow-wood, Green Ash, Siberian Crab-apple
4, 40% — Horse-chestnut, Catalpa, Kentucky Coffee-tree
5, 20% — European White Birch, Poplars, Black Locust

As an illustration, let us select two trees of equal size from the Eastern Region for a monetary value comparison. Assuming that both trees have a trunk diameter of 20 inches at breast height, each would have 314 square inches in cross section. This is the diameter in inches, squared, then multiplied by .7854 ($20 \times 20 = 400 \times .7854 = 314$). The basic value, figured at $6.00 per square inch is therefore $1884.

If a red oak were one of the trees, its basic value would be $1884 since it is in Class 1, which is rated 100%. Then, if this red oak were in perfect condition and were also an important plant in relationship to the house, the value would not change. The final evaluation would therefore be $1884.

Selecting as the other tree a Carolina poplar, which is in Class 5 with a rating of 20%, the value would immediately drop from the basic value of $1884 to $376 ($1884 × 20%). If the physical condition of the tree were rated 60%, its value would then be $225 ($376 × 60%). And if the landscape placement of the tree were rated 80%, the final evaluation of this poplar would be $180 ($225 × 80%). This is considerably less than the valuation of the red oak of the same size.

The formula should be considered flexible. A tree might be listed in Class 2 or in Class 3, for instance, yet be an exceptionally fine specimen or have some historical significance. An appraiser would therefore be justified in giving it a higher percentage rating than the charts designate.

PART TWO
A Variety of Forms

CHAPTER 6

Small Trees for Flowers and Foliage

In this day of smaller houses, limited planting areas, and more intimate terraces and courts, there is a vastly increased demand for small ornamental trees. Those that do not exceed 20 or 30 feet in height are most highly prized. They fulfill the need for trees without overwhelming house and grounds with their shade. Even when planted some distance from the house, they offer an enhancing texture variant to the commonly used evergreen foundation planting.

And when the small flowering trees burst into bloom, they are like gorgeous bouquets. Since they have thousands of blossoms, a few of their branches can be cut carefully with pruning shears for indoor decoration without in any way diminishing the outdoor display.

Then, too, there are a number of small trees that, while having no bright flowers, are notable for other features; it disturbs me to find so many of these passed over. Interesting leaf pattern, colorful fall foliage, a trunk of unusual color, and even a neat branching system on a dependable tree are all worthy of more of our attention.

Leaves for Pattern

One particular leaf shape is associated with the maple, and yet with all the species there are, each maple has a wonderfully designed pattern of its own. An entire chapter could be devoted to a host of small maples, mostly of Asiatic origin, but I will limit myself to four.

The Japanese maple has seven long pointed lobes that are deeply incised, giving a clear-cut silhouette. Observe a single branch with a dozen or so leaves against the sky, or better yet, see it as a shadow against a wall, and you will realize why the designers

53

of Japan like to incorporate this outline into their art work. It is the red-leaved form of the Japanese maple that is almost invariably seen in this country. Leaves of the original species are green, and its pleasantly neutral tone makes it a plant of even greater usefulness in many landscapes. In the fall its leaves turn a more brilliant color than those which have been red throughout the summer.

Trident maple has three lobes, the center one being somewhat longer than the others. The foliage is dark green and glossy. Late in the season it turns a dark red and the glossiness of the leaf intensifies its fall color. This maple is too little known at the present time.

The leaf of the paperbark maple is also three-parted, and its fuzziness gives it further interest. The tree's most noticeable characteristic, however, is its bark. Portions of it are smooth, while other sections are covered with paper-thin strips. The bark's orange-brown color is particularly striking during the winter months.

The hedge maple is native to Europe. Unlike the other species, it has rounded lobes that are not deeply cut. It is a neat, compact tree that requires no pruning to make it appropriate for small areas.

As for two non-maples with interesting leaves, there is the American holly, a broad-leaved evergreen. Selected forms with their dark green leathery leaves are handsome—and, of course, closely associated with the Christmas season. And hardy-orange has not only fragrant flowers and attractive fruits but also a deep green trifoliate leaf on green twigs with conspicuous green thorns.

Flowering Trees for Gaiety

The first color masses of the spring season are provided by shadblow, magnolia, and peach. When most plants bear not even a hint of green foliage, these trees are full blown, a welcome sight indeed.

Allegheny shadblow has white flowers that seem intensified because they are set off by unfolding leaves of bronzy red tones. The smooth gray bark is attractive in winter.

The star magnolia has large, fragrant blossoms with many narrow petals of a pure, glistening white. The flower buds are encased in fuzzy scales, somewhat like those of the pussy willow, to protect them from winter cold. These attributes, plus excellent foliage and a smooth trunk, give this tree a year-round high rating.

Some trees are worth growing solely for their handsome bouquets. The double white flowering peach is an example of such: the tree itself is not considered shapely and is rather short lived. Among the flowering peaches, there are also double pinks, one light and one dark, for variation.

Saucer magnolia next delights us with its magnificent flowers, which come out before its leaves. The flowers are primarily white but the outer petals carry some pink or reddish purple that sets them off in style. There are several named varieties of which the late-flowering Lennei is very choice. It has a rich, reddish purple coloring, and the thick petals are held firmly upright in strong, sculptural lines.

Saucer Magnolia is bold in design. It is fitting for use near large buildings. (*George Taloumis*)

Mid-spring sets off a mass of bloom, among which crab-apples, cherries, redbud, silverbell, and dogwood are the old reliables.

We have the Orient to thank for the many flowering crab-apples that we plant today. The first ones were introduced to this country more than a century ago. We still plant some of the original types, but they have been augmented by numerous hybrids. The current trend is toward the deeper colors, the reds and the magentas. A greater use of more of the whites, near-whites, and light pinks would provide some contrast to the reds of the species and to the bright colors of other plants that come into bloom at the same time. Moreover, the lighter shades harmonize better with a greater variety of house colors.

The small flower of the redbud appears in large numbers all along the twigs, and an occasional blossom can even be found on very old branches. Although the native plant has a blossom of magenta, there is an excellent white variety as well as a new pink selection.

Flowering dogwood deserves its popularity, not only for its beauty but also for the long-lasting quality of its white or pink spring display. The showy bracts, being less fragile than true petals, stay on for several weeks despite heavy rains or strong winds.

Carolina silverbell has white bell-shaped flowers almost an inch long. Four fins on the dried fruit make them look like depth bombs.

The large, double, deep bluish pink blossom of Kwanzan flowering cherry is much admired, and this tree is quite generally available. Not as easy to find but certainly worth searching for are related varieties with light pink or white flowers. Nevertheless, the double-flowered varieties do keep their blossoms longer; they are not so easily dislodged by rain or wind.

Fortunately, not all of the spring flowering trees are on display at the same time. Several follow a week or two after the early burst of color. Goldenchain, the hardiest of the laburnums, is one of these. Its long clusters of deep yellow flowers display gracefully.

Paul's scarlet hawthorn has a double, deep pink flower. Several leaf diseases spoil the effectiveness of this tree along the eastern seaboard, but in other areas it is highly regarded.

The sweet-bay magnolia has a 3-inch white flower which turns a rich creamy color before it drops. It doesn't have a mass of flowers at any one time, but after its late spring showing it provides the surprise of scattered flowers throughout the summer.

SUMMER FLOWERS

June and bloom are synonymous in the poet's notebook but they gain little support among the flowering tree group. However, there are four plants of good quality that wait until this time of year to blossom forth.

Japanese snowbell is the first of the June-flowering trees to make its appearance. The white flowers shaped like little bells are curved back sharply and give a dainty Japanesque character to the plant.

Since the native flowering dogwood is so well known, one might think that the Japanese dogwood would be seen more frequently than it is, and yet it has only recently begun to come into the trade. It blooms when the bracts start to drop from the native species. The Japanese dogwood's white bracts are long pointed and they last for several weeks.

The Japanese tree lilac has large clusters of creamy white flowers. But admirers of the common lilac who anticipate a similar fragrance from this plant will be in for a disappointment, because its aroma is not pleasant at close range. It is, however, a striking tree when in bloom and its dark green summer foliage is noteworthy.

Many a good tree continues to remain virtually unknown. The Korean stewartia belongs to this overlooked group. It has a rather large single white flower similar in shape to a single-flowered camellia. Its mottled leaf in the fall is most unusual, and the flaking varicolored bark of its older trees is especially noticeable after the foliage has dropped.

July is not without flowers, thanks to the goldenrain-tree, silk-tree, and sorrel-tree.

The goldenrain-tree has small yellow flowers of deep color; although they fall quickly, the interesting swollen seed pods remain on the tree for a long time. The fruits change in color from light green to pink to brown.

The silk-tree's flower, produced over a period of several weeks, is unique. The numerous thread-like pink stamens give the appearance of a dainty powder puff. Many small leaflets combine to make up each large leaf, the over-all effect being that of a graceful tropical plant.

Sorrel-tree has pendulous clusters of white flowers. The light-colored stem and seed cluster contrast with the bright red glossy leaf in early fall.

In late September, franklinia displays its 3-inch single white flowers with their yellow stamens. The foliage turns to bright orange and red later in the autumn.

Showy Fruits

Brightly colored fruits remain showy for a longer period than do the more fragile flowers; so when a plant is noted for both a floral and a fruit display, we are given an extra treat.

The many kinds of crab-apple produce fruits in quantity, some red, others yellow. For the most part they are not much more than half an inch in diameter.

Flowering dogwood has clusters of bright red fruit while the Japanese dogwood has a large strawberry-like fruit that is completely different.

The several magnolias start with green fruits that resemble a knobby cucumber. The fruits turn red as they ripen; then small sections open to reveal bright red seeds which are fastened to the core with thin white elastic threads.

The American holly's red fruits often last throughout the winter. Silverbell, goldenrain-tree, sorrel-tree, and hardy-orange display distinctive fruits.

The red fruits of the cockspur and Washington hawthorns are much more striking than their small white flowers and offer an attractive display after the leaves have fallen. Both these trees have lustrous foliage which turns orange-scarlet in the autumn.

Interesting Bark

Bark is usually thought of simply as a functional part of the tree and is largely overlooked when ornamental qualities are considered. But a number of trees have outstanding bark that becomes especially noticeable during the winter and early spring months. Small trees are well represented in this group. Allegheny shadblow and star and saucer magnolia have smooth bark of light color that takes on a new sheen under a winter sun. Japanese dogwood has a mottled bark of several subdued colors, and as irregular patches of old bark drop off, light-colored areas are revealed. Paperbark maple with its unusual orange-brown coloring cannot help but attract attention.

European hornbeam and hop hornbeam are both members of the birch family, though they resemble other trees. The European species has a smooth gray bark similar to that of a small beech. The hop hornbeam, native to the United States, has a bark of thin, narrow, flaky sections.

Small Trees Listed According to Hardiness [1]

See Zones of Hardiness Map (frontispiece).
(*) Better adapted to southern sector of zone.

Hardiness Zone 4: –30 to –20 degrees: Flowering Crab-apple, Allegheny Shadblow.

Hardiness Zone 5: –20 to –10 degrees: Flowering Dogwood, Japanese Dogwood(*), Waterer Goldenchain(*), Cockspur Hawthorn, Paul's Scarlet Hawthorn, Washington Hawthorn, European Hornbeam, Hop Hornbeam, Japanese Tree Lilac, Saucer Magnolia(*), Star Magnolia(*), Sweet-bay Magnolia(*), Hedge Maple, Eastern Redbud(*), Carolina Silverbell, Sorrel-tree.

---

[1] For descriptions, cultural notes, and botanical names of these trees, see Chapter 15.

Hardiness Zone 6: −10 to 0 degrees: Kwanzan Flowering Cherry(*), Franklinia(*), Goldenrain-tree, Hardy-orange(*), American Holly, Japanese Maple, Paperbark Maple, Trident Maple, Double White Flowering Peach, Japanese Snowbell, Korean Stewartia.

Hardiness Zone 7: 0 to 10 degrees: Silk-tree.

CHAPTER 7

Small Shade Trees

When we think of shade trees, large plants such as sugar maples, red oaks, honey-locusts, and sweet-gums come quickly to mind. If asked to name a few that do not grow as tall, we generally think of small flowering trees such as dogwood, crab-apple, and magnolia. Rarely are shade trees of intermediate size mentioned.

Yet today, with our more compact homes, there is a need for trees that do not have the dimensions of forest giants and yet are large enough to offer shade for our lawns and outdoor living areas and tall enough to provide a setting for our houses. Trees that at maturity will be between 30 and 50 feet in height meet this requirement.

There are easily a dozen deciduous trees in this size category, some of which combine the flowering beauty of the small trees with the branching habit of the large.

And these medium-sized trees have the advantage of low maintenance cost, especially where spraying and pruning are concerned.

Extended Seasonal Interest

The contribution of these trees to our pleasure and well-being does not stop with summertime shade. We live in a four-season part of the world and many of our trees have extended seasonal interests. The Bradford pear, for example, has showy white flowers in the spring, glossy dark green leaves in summer, and then in late autumn, after many other trees have lost their leaves, its foliage takes on deep rich red tones. Its small fruits will not litter a lawn, and it is resistant to the pests which normally affect the standard-sized pears.

The yellow-wood with its white flowers displayed in long wisteria-like clusters in early summer is an eye stopper. Its fall color is a

Yellow-wood is a small shade tree with long clusters of white flowers in June. Its smooth gray bark offers interest at all times of the year. (*Paul E. Genereux*)

sunny yellow. Equally important is its winter interest. The uncommonly smooth bark of light gray has a distinct appeal.

Other flowering plants in this group which offer at least two seasons of interest are Chinese scholar-tree, Siberian crab-apple, Korean mountain-ash, European mountain-ash, Sargent cherry, mountain silverbell, and Hokkaido magnolia.

The Chinese scholar-tree has creamy flowers in August when a floral display by a woody plant is a rarity. It is one of the last of the trees to shed its leaves, and they remain green until they fall. Then the numerous green seed pods, which are constricted and not unlike a necklace, give a leaf-like appearance on the green twigs.

The Siberian crab-apple is the tallest member of the crab-apple group. Its white flowers appear ten days ahead of the others, and in early fall its yellow, or sometimes red, fruits are displayed.

The Korean mountain-ash does not have as showy fruit as the much more commonly seen European mountain-ash, but it more than makes up for this by being less subject to borers and leaf-chewing insects and by its attractive yellow fall coloring and its smooth gray bark.

The European mountain-ash is well known for its large clusters of bright orange-red berries in late summer and early fall. Its white flower cluster is also attractive.

The Sargent cherry is the tallest member of its clan. Although its flowers are not as large or long lasting as many related species, they are quickly followed by colorful leaves which start as pinkish bronze, are green during the summer, and then in the autumn turn a lively orange-red that adds sparkle to any landscape.

Mountain silverbell becomes a taller specimen than the more common Carolina silverbell. The white bell-like flowers arranged along the twigs are interesting, and the seed pod with its four fins is distinctive.

Hokkaido magnolia has large white flowers in early spring. Its summer foliage is typical of the genus, and that means top quality. It is the tallest of the showy-flowered deciduous magnolias, for it eventually reaches 50 feet.

Foliage and Form

Three small shade trees that cannot lay claim to showy flowers or fruit gain a good rating by the excellent quality of their leaves and their shapely form. Little-leaf European linden, willow oak, and katsura possess a certain dignity that gives them a noble air.

The little-leaf European linden is the most commonly used of the three, and its small, rounded leaf of dark green, together with its compact form, give it a degree of formality that befits many a planting.

Willow oak has dense branching and fine-textured narrow leaves, features not associated with the oaks. Again unlike most oaks, it is easily transplanted.

The katsura is seldom seen, and one cannot but wonder why, for it is a good choice for a garden or other area of limited size. Its small, rounded leaves on fine twigs help to give it a neat appearance. The young unfolding leaves afford a subtle blending of muted reds and delicate yellows that when seen against a blue sky are as handsome as flowers. In the autumn the foliage turns a golden yellow.

Trees for Adverse Conditions

The areas we have to plant are not always favored with the best of growing conditions. In such instances, we should consider selecting a rugged plant. In the medium-sized group there are two from which to choose: Amur cork-tree and sawtooth oak.

The Amur cork-tree will grow where the soil is dry and where the air may be polluted, or at least where it is not country-fresh. Its leaf is compound, usually of five to eleven leaflets. The thick spongy bark of a mature specimen is most unusual.

Most of the oaks are upland trees and do well with a minimum of moisture. The rarely seen sawtooth oak is no exception. The leaf differs from that of the typical oak in that it is not lobed; it is elliptical and toothed, like the leaf of a chestnut.

Small Shade Trees Listed According to Hardiness [1]

See Zones of Hardiness Map (frontispiece).
(*) Better adapted to southern sector of zone.

Hardiness Zone 3: −40 to −30 degrees: Amur Cork-tree(*), Siberian Crab-apple, European Mountain-ash.

Hardiness Zone 4: −30 to −20 degrees: Katsura(*), Little-leaf Linden(*), Korean Mountain-ash.

[1] For descriptions, cultural notes, and botanical names of these trees, see Chapter 15.

Hardiness Zone 5: −20 to −10 degrees: Hokkaido Magnolia, Chinese Scholar-tree(*), Mountain Silverbell(*), Yellow-wood(*).

Hardiness Zone 6: −10 to 0 degrees: Sargent Cherry, Sawtooth Oak, Willow Oak(*), Bradford Pear.

CHAPTER 8

Large Shade Trees

Large-sized shade trees are an important part of our heritage and some of our most widely admired trees are to be found among them. A survey of officially designated State Trees shows that more have been selected from this group than from any other, though evergreens in the same size category run a close second.

The large shade tree may be thought of as one that at maturity will range in height from 50 to 100 feet.

A high-branched, deciduous tree provides desired shade during the warmer months, and then, during the winter, drops its foliage, and so no longer blocks out the sun's rays when daylight hours are shorter and we are in need of more light.

Many people feel that, whatever its attributes, a leafless tree has lost its attractiveness. But the artist, with his sensitivity and trained eye, is apt to consider the bare tree of winter more attention-arresting than one in full leaf, because of the pattern of the branches, the structural form, the everchanging shadows on the trunk, on the ground, and on nearby buildings and walls.

A Quartet for Fall Color

Sugar maple, sweet-gum, pepperidge, ginkgo—what a fall color spectacular! These trees can be seen from miles away as they paint a hillside in the gayest of colors or they can be admired at close range, even along a city street. Yet with all its brilliance, the display is in no sense gaudy. The individual leaf, too, with its subtle, complex blending of colors is worthy of study. Though these trees rate well at any time of the year, it is in autumn that they come to our attention in a conspicuous way; they belong to a tree nobility and carry their colors with pride.

Sugar Maple is a sturdy tree whose brilliant autumn color brightens the landscape. (*George Taloumis*)

The sugar maple does not grow naturally under all conditions; therefore, when we plant it we should use some discretion. It prefers the country atmosphere to that of the city, and it needs space in which to spread its branches. The fall color of some of these trees is yellow-orange while that of others is pure yellow.

Ginkgo, a tree that belongs to the ages, has a long and entertaining history. It is indeed a living fossil since its unique leaf imprint has been found on ancient rocks. The golden color of its autumn foliage glistens brightly for several days, then the leaves all drop at about the same time, but even on the ground they retain their lively color for a short period.

The pepperidge (also called sour-gum or tupelo) is not by nature found in large groves. It grows as an isolated specimen or, at most, in small groups. Since it does not take well to transplanting, this singular tree is usually seen in its natural state rather than under cultivation. Its branching habit is rugged and outstanding. In the early fall the foliage turns a dark red, and this color combined with the high gloss of the leaf creates unusual brilliance.

The sweet-gum is late to show its autumn colors but they are worth waiting for—reds, yellows, purples, greens, all on one leaf, a beautiful mosaic. Add to this the good structure of the tree and its clean-cut summer foliage and you can easily understand why it is highly rated.

Colorful Bark—Stately Form

Birch, beech, and London plane with their light-colored bark are attractive at all times, but in the winter and early spring they are particularly impressive. Magnolias, linden, tulip-tree, and Norway maple have a different type of distinction, one of quiet dignity that comes from their stately form.

The bark of the paper birch is the whitest of whites. Older sections of the outer bark peel off in long strips. The slender twigs and natural gracefulness of this birch have earned it the name of "Lady of the Woods."

Bark of light gray distinguishes the American beech from its European relative, which is several shades darker. The European beech, however, is more readily available to us from nurseries.

And its many horticultural forms have appealed to the public, the purple- or copper-leaved variety especially.

London plane is the tree of the city street where it has flourished under less than ideal conditions. Its bark is darker than that of the native sycamore, or plane, of which it is a hybrid, but the sycamore does not take as kindly to man-made settings. In either tree, the flaking, mottled bark is of interest.

The Norway maple is another tree that has been widely planted in cities and even more widely in the suburbs. It has a dense crown of dark foliage that lends stateliness. Its dense shade and surface roots offer considerable competition to an adjacent lawn.

Southern magnolia is widely known and greatly admired wherever it can be grown. The large, dark green glossy leaves give it distinction. The related cucumber-tree, which is much, much hardier, is not as familiar. Yet it, too, has a majestic form. Its foliage is not as glossy, its flowers are greenish and not especially noticeable; nevertheless, this magnolia deserves to be better known.

Dark green above, silvery on the underside: that sets apart the leaf of the silver linden. The tree is as uniformly shaped as if a master pruner had been at work. Again we have a tree that, while seldom seen, should become more widely planted and enjoyed.

The tulip-tree with its distinctively notched leaf and unique flower appeals to all who have studied native flora. Its long, straight trunk and shapely top attract the eye. Like several other native trees, it does not transplant well and is not generally found at garden centers. Small plants are sometimes offered for sale and these are most satisfactory. The tulip-tree grows more rapidly than most trees and in a few years becomes an imposing specimen.

The Oaks, the Elms, and Substitutes

The oak is the symbol of sturdiness, and it lives up to its reputation. Its branching structure and the soundness of its wood give this tree the strength to resist storms.

Red and pin oak are two of the most widely planted of this

genus. Both have good green summer foliage and in autumn both turn a deep red. The red oak is better along a street since it does not have the down-sweeping branches of the pin oak. One reason for the popularity of the pin oak is that it is the fastest-growing member of this group. The leaf of the scarlet oak is midway between that of the red and the pin oak, but because the tree is rather difficult to transplant, it has not been commonly planted. Its glossy foliage accentuates its fall color.

Because the leaf of the shingle oak is not lobed, many would not recognize this rarely planted tree even if they happened to see it. As a matter of fact, its shiny leaf resembles that of the mountain-laurel. But it is one of the smaller trees of the oak group and because of its deep-rooting habit qualifies as a good lawn tree.

The white oak is a rugged tree that looks best as a single specimen on a rocky hillside or in a large lawn area. It is one of the more difficult trees to transplant and is very slow-growing, hence is infrequently planted. But where one exists on a property, it is almost invariably considered to be a choice possession.

Few trees have the sentimental appeal of the American elm. Many of the historic trees associated with Colonial days were elms. It was one of the most easily transplanted of trees and its arches have graced many a street. However, in recent years it has had more than its share of troubles, and as of the present moment there is no certain control for the deadly Dutch elm disease and phloem necrosis that have selected it as their principal target. Research continues, and it is hoped that some day a reliable and practical cure will be found.

Many people want a substitute for the elm—a usable tree that to some degree, at least, resembles an elm. Zelkova is a possible answer. Although it is not widely known, it has been around this country for at least a hundred years. It is closely related to the elm and has shown a resistance to the diseases that beset the latter. It has a smaller leaf and better fall color, muted red.

The thornless honey-locust is another possibility. It can be trained as a high-branched tree, and the openness of its foliage permits light to penetrate to the lawn below. Unlike most trees,

Zelkova has been suggested as a substitute for the elm. Its small leaves, fine twigs, and muted red autumn color combine to make it a desirable specimen. (*Edward H. Scanlon & Associates*)

it presents no leaf raking problem in the fall, for its small leaflets curl up and disintegrate.

Large Shade Trees Listed According to Hardiness [1]

See Zones of Hardiness Map (frontispiece).
(*) Better adapted to southern sector of zone.

Hardiness Zone 2: –50 to –40 degrees: Paper Birch, American Elm.

Hardiness Zone 4: –30 to –20 degrees: American Beech(*), Ginkgo(*), Thornless Honey-locust(*), Silver Linden, Norway Maple, Sugar Maple, Red Oak(*), Scarlet Oak(*), White Oak.

Hardiness Zone 5: –20 to –10 degrees: European Beech, Cucumber-tree, Pin Oak, Shingle Oak, Pepperidge, London Plane(*), Tulip-tree, Zelkova(*).

Hardiness Zone 6: –10 to 0 degrees: Sweet-gum.

Hardiness Zone 7: 0 to 10 degrees: Southern Magnolia(*).

---

[1] For descriptions, cultural notes, and botanical names of these trees, see Chapter 15.

CHAPTER 9

Evergreen Trees from 20 to 80 Feet

The needle evergreens, or conifers, hold particular appeal during the winter months although they play an important part in landscape design at other times as well. In the spring and again in the fall, they offer a fine background for seasonal bursts of color, the brilliant displays appearing even more vivid against their dark greens. During the summer the variation in texture offered by the narrow-leaved evergreens is a nice contrast to those of deciduous plants. All the evergreens have an aroma that we associate with the pure air of the mountains.

Mistakes have been made in the use of needle evergreens. And what may be a minor error of judgment in placing a deciduous tree becomes a major error with a tree that has the year-round density of the conifers. The problem arises because trees are usually planted when they are only a few feet in height. Since a small evergreen appears to be a finished specimen, we are likely to assume that it will retain its size indefinitely—but it grows and grows and grows.

Not all conifers belong to the forest-giant class and some fine ones can be picked from those that are smaller in size. We simply need to use caution in our choice and in our placement.

Columnar Evergreens for Small Areas

Columnar trees give desired height without taking up much ground space. (Discussion of deciduous columnars will be found in Chapter 10.)

Cryptomeria, umbrella-pine, and Swiss stone pine are columnar evergreens which are not usually seen. They are complete strangers even to many who know a large number of trees.

The foliage of cryptomeria resembles that of the California

sequoia but in size it is more like the red-cedar. It is at its best in areas that are only a few miles from the sea.

Umbrella-pine has distinctive foliage: long, flat needles arranged in large whorls. There is a glossiness to the needle that is unusual in a conifer. Though very different in appearance from other plants, the umbrella-pine may properly be used in the most refined of settings.

Of these three plants, the Swiss stone pine is the most columnar in form. It has the soft needle of the white pine but is more compact.

Red-cedar and American arborvitae are natives that have long been used. To insure getting plants that will retain a good green color at all seasons, it is best to obtain selections that have been propagated vegetatively; that is, by grafting or cuttings.

Two closely related plants that represent horticultural selections offer a variation in color and form. Blue columnar Chinese juniper has silvery green foliage, and, unlike the native red-cedar, it does not act as a host for the cedar-apple rust. The pyramidal form of American arborvitae is a smaller columnar plant than the normal species. It is faster growing and less expensive than other evergreens of this shape.

Small Evergreens

There are dwarf varieties of all the common evergreen trees, but these may be considered as rare, slow-growing shrubs that are better suited to a rock garden or to a specialty garden than to use as small trees.

There are other evergreens of limited size. I refer to upright Japanese yew, mugo pine, and Tanyosho pine. These can be considered as small trees with multiple stems, and they will become a prized part of the garden picture.

Upright Japanese yew is so commonly used as a tightly sheared plant that it is difficult to think of it as tree-like with a 3- to 6-inch trunk. The reddish brown trunk and branches are nicely set off by the dark green foliage.

Dwarf forms of the mugo pine are more generally seen than is the tree type. The latter is a spreading plant with short, dark green needles. It will give firmness to a design that might be composed predominantly of fine-textured plants.

Tanyosho pine is slow growing, which is why it is not a favorite of commercial growers. Mature plants are as wide as they are high, and with several stems from the base they offer a sculptural effect.

Evergreens of Intermediate Size

Several conifers grow to a size that compares well with the small deciduous shade trees discussed in Chapter 7. Because of their restricted size, they fit the great majority of present-day homesites. And many of them have interesting colors.

Blue Atlas Cedar has a soft blue color and a pleasantly informal branching habit. As with other evergreen trees, it is best to place it at some distance from the house. (*Roche*)

I know we associate greenness rather than color with the conifers, but still the blue Atlas cedar and the silver Japanese white pine have distinctively colored needles while the Scotch and the lace-bark pine have bark of outstanding color.

The blue Atlas cedar has a silvery blue cast to its needles that sets it apart from other trees. It is open branching and does not have the severe lines that we associate with the spruces.

The silver Japanese white pine's darker color is not quite as striking, but the tree itself is a much hardier one than the blue Atlas cedar. Then, too, it has irregular, spreading branches which give it a picturesque form.

The upper branches and trunk of a mature Scotch pine have an orange-brown color that contrasts with its blue-green needles. Older specimens are quite open, and their orange-brown bark viewed against a blue sky is attractive.

The rare lace-bark pine has a unique feature. Its bark flakes off like that of the sycamore. The trunks of older trees are almost white.

Three others in the intermediate size group are noted for their dark foliage: Japanese black pine, Japanese hemlock, and Carolina hemlock.

Japanese black pine, like many plants from Japan, does well near the seashore. This tree is noted also for its irregular outline. It has long been a favorite of garden designers in the Orient.

The Japanese hemlock is more compact than the commonly used Canada hemlock and does not grow as tall or as fast. Possibly if it were more widely available it would be used more frequently—and the hedge shears would be given a bit of a rest.

The Carolina hemlock is somewhat irregular in its branching, and some specimens produce a lacy effect that is pleasing.

Evergreens for Large Areas

Pine, spruce, fir, and hemlock are well known, especially the larger members of each genus. With the exception of the hemlock, they do not lend themselves to restrictive pruning for height control.

The smallest needles and the most slender twigs of this large tree group belong to the Canada hemlock. At least in part for these reasons, it is well adapted to pruning and can be kept to one-quarter its normal size while still retaining the character of an informal tree. Yearly pruning is required, however, and should be started while the tree is still small.

Spruce and fir are noted for their sharply pointed conical shape. The Colorado spruce is the most severe in outline. It presents a dense mass of foliage and looks best when the lower branches are allowed to remain. Such a tree takes up more area than is available on small properties.

The Norway spruce has more space between branches and is noted for the pendulous habit of its branchlets. Where it grows well it is a graceful tree; but, again, it is one that requires much space and should be used with discretion.

Less well known is the white fir. It has silver-green foliage and in this respect compares with the Colorado blue spruce. However, in my opinion it is in all respects superior, less harsh in color and outline, and less subject to attack by insects.

Douglas-fir, native to the northwestern United States, is a fine evergreen for landscaping, since it is less wide spreading than many others. For the Eastern states, a form originating in the Rocky Mountains will grow more successfully than the tree from coastal regions.

Most pines have wide-spreading branches, but since they lose the lower ones they are not as massive as other conifers. The white pine, in particular, has spreading horizontal branches that give it a pleasing informality. Its needles are soft to the touch, and the color and general appearance emphasize this sense of softness.

Austrian pine is a darker color and has a more rigid needle. It offers a bolder mass to the landscape scene.

Evergreen Trees Listed According to Hardiness [1]

See Zones of Hardiness Map (frontispiece).
(*) Better adapted to southern sector of zone.

Hardiness Zone 3: –40 to –30 degrees: American Arborvitae, Pyramidal Arborvitae, Douglas-fir(*), Canada Hemlock, Eastern White Pine(*), Mugo Pine, Scotch Pine, Swiss Stone Pine, Red-cedar, Colorado Spruce, Norway Spruce.

Hardiness Zone 4: –30 to –20 degrees: White Fir, Blue Columnar Chinese Juniper, Austrian Pine.

Hardiness Zone 5: –20 to –10 degrees: Carolina Hemlock, Japanese Black Pine, Lace-bark Pine, Tanyosho Pine, Upright Japanese Yew.

Hardiness Zone 6: –10 to 0 degrees: Cryptomeria, Japanese Hemlock, Silver Japanese White Pine, Umbrella-pine.

Hardiness Zone 7: 0 to 10 degrees: Blue Atlas Cedar.

[1] For descriptions, cultural notes, and botanical names of these trees, see Chapter 15.

CHAPTER 10

Columnar, Pendulous, Colored-foliage Trees

In my student days I was taught that weeping and contorted trees and plants with colored foliage were bizarre, in poor taste; that they came in and went out with the overly ornate Victorian houses. Gardens of the late nineteenth century did make use of them, and they were spotted around the front lawns in great variety. People of that generation had not heard of status symbols, but the captains of industry had ways of showing that they had acquired wealth, and one of those ways was by putting several unusual plants where passersby would be sure to notice them.

More recently, good modern designers have recognized that many of these plants taken individually have a bold sculptured look; that they can be used to add a dramatic note against plain surfaces. The contemporary landscape artist has learned to use striking figures with restraint.

One plant or several of the same kind can be employed with stunning effectiveness, but where these unusual forms are seen in mixed combinations, the conflict of interest creates a jarring note. Thus such types are at their best as an integral part of the complete design. They are difficult to use well along a street of small homes because the trees and houses compete with each other for attention.

Columnar Trees

Columnar trees can be used in numbers as a tall screen at the edge of an area, or they can be placed individually near a building to provide contrast to the horizontal line of the structure. As we noted earlier, their distinct advantage is that they require little space.

Lombardy poplar is likely to come to mind when columnar trees are mentioned; but it is out of favor today since its naturally short life is made even more so by a serious canker disease of the trunk. Its root system also proves troublesome. About the only reason for selecting it is its inexpensiveness and the fast rate of growth which makes it useful as a temporary planting. Fortunately, there are a host of far better plants to choose from.

Large deciduous columnar forms can be purchased in three varieties of maple, in a beech, a birch, and an oak.

The erect Norway maple has dark green leaves, and since it is comparatively narrow it does not shade a lawn excessively as the regular Norway maple does. Columnar sugar maple is slower to become established but does offer the bonus of good fall color. Scanlon maple is broadly columnar and again gives color in the autumn.

The pyramidal English oak is a rugged tree with dark green foliage. Like other oaks, it is a long-lived tree that is well thought of by plantsmen. The English oaks do not take on the striking autumn colors of our native species.

The Dawyck beech is a select form of the European beech. It is fastigiate; that is to say, the side branches parallel the central leader. The smooth gray bark gives winter interest.

Columnar white birch is also a variety of a European tree. Its white bark offers a pleasing contrast to a dark background.

Frequently we have need for a small columnar tree. We might choose from among three such: the European hornbeam, the hawthorn, and the Amanogawa flowering cherry.

The pyramidal European hornbeam has smooth, dark gray bark and looks something like a small beech. Since it responds to trimming very well, its size can be further restricted.

Columnar hawthorn is a dense, narrow, upright plant. White flowers, red fruit, and autumn color of foliage are worthwhile extras.

The delicate pink, semi-double flowers of Amanogawa flowering cherry make it one of the finest of the numerous varieties of regular flowering cherries. It is the only cherry that is both small and columnar.

Columnar trees can be used for accent or as a tall screen if space is limited. The Pyramidal English Oak is a long-lived tree with deep roots. (*Paul E. Genereux*)

In the intermediate size we find a trio of flowering trees that are narrow and upright:

Columnar Sargent cherry has single pink flowers in the spring; the leaves turn a lively yellow-orange in the autumn.

Columnar Siberian crab-apple has white flowers early in the spring and small red fruits in the fall. Its upper branches should be trimmed to prevent a broad top from developing; otherwise the weight of heavy fruiting may spoil the shape of the tree.

Wilson columnar mountain-ash offers fastigiate branching which results in a dense upright form. White flowers and bright orange berries add to its outstanding appearance.

Pendulous Branches

Weeping trees can be obtained in large size or small. Most of them are grown for the graceful effect of their long pendulous branches. Some have springtime flowers and autumn fruits for added attractiveness.

The weeping Japanese cherry is a cascade of delicate pink when in flower. Both single- and double-flowered forms are available.

Red Jade crab-apple is a patented plant that is relatively new. It has numerous white flowers, but it is not until late autumn that it really comes into its own: the small, bright red fruits on the long, slender, pendulous twigs are a beautiful sight.

The Sargent weeping hemlock is usually grown as a spreading, fountain-like shrub. However, it can be staked to make it develop into a narrow, pendulous tree.

Camperdown elm is a small tree with a bold form, instead of the graceful one of other weeping trees. As a result, it fits well near massive buildings. It has, however, lost some of its popularity in recent years because it is difficult to combine with other plants and also because it is subject to the serious elm diseases.

Of the large pendulous trees, weeping willow is the best known. Its branches will touch the ground. It looks well when grown near a small lake. But it is subject to trunk canker and other pests, although in some sections of the country canker is not prevalent. And it is one of the fast-growing plants, with all of their virtues and faults. (See Chapter 11.)

Even though the cutleaf European birch has slender twigs that droop, it does not have the unusually marked weeping habit of the weeping willow. The small cut leaf and the white trunk convey a feeling of lightness.

Weeping beech trees were used on great estates in years gone by, and now these are collectors' items used in large commercial developments. The gray bark, the sculptured effect of the branches, and the longevity of the tree add to its value. Some plants are wide spreading, others are narrow. The latter are usually considered the more desirable. Weeping beech is not an easy tree to move; the process requires experienced plantsmen.

Contorted and Globe Shapes

Several trees have spirally shaped branches which in some cases are combined with pendulous twigs. Frequently these are so oddly shaped as to become freakish.

The contorted Hankow willow is one of the most useful trees of this type. Its twigs and even larger branches have a well-defined corkscrew effect, but not a pendulous habit. The winter silhouette is particularly diverting.

There are a number of globe-shaped trees but only one will be considered here—the globe Norway maple. It grows 15 to 20 feet in height and retains a compact, globe-shaped top. No pruning is necessary to maintain this size or shape.

Colored Foliage

Trees whose foliage is of a dark red or reddish purple color throughout the summer are outstanding, but because they are so different from trees with normally green foliage, they should be placed with great care. It is best to group several plants of one kind together. The practice of alternating colored-foliage plants with normally green varieties is not recommended.

Copper beech and related varieties may be the best of the colored-foliage group. Prize specimens are not uncommon on old estates. Since they are wide-spreading trees, they need space to develop properly. Rivers beech is a selection of a darker color.

Among Norway maples, Fassens Black and the somewhat lighter colored Crimson King are selections that retain a deep reddish leaf during the summer. They have all but replaced the Schwedler maple, the leaves of which are quite red in late spring but turn to a normal green during the summer. By the way, some dealers feel that the name Fassens Black does not have popular appeal so they call their trees Fassens Red.

Bloodleaf Japanese maple is a small tree with red foliage. The color is kept summer-long if the tree is grown in full sun.

There are a number of purple-leaved plums as represented by Thundercloud. The tree is comparable in size to the Japanese maple but the leaf is darker and more of a purple; the tree is hardier, also.

Welch flowering dogwood has a mottled leaf of pale green, cream, and light red. In the autumn these colors become intensified.

Sunburst honey-locust has on its outer twigs bright yellow leaflets which make this tree stand out like a beacon. This appeals to some people. Others feel that while such a color display is attractive for a short period in the autumn, as a steady summer diet it can become tiresome.

Gray or blue-green foliage offers a good neutral foil for bright colors, but even these colors need to be used with care.

Colorado blue spruce, for example, is admired by many. It is difficult to use on small properties because considerable ground space is required to do it justice. Furthermore, its blue tone often fails to harmonize with adjacent plants.

Blue Atlas cedar is softer of color and of outline than the spruce. It is naturally a large, wide-spreading tree but it can be restrained somewhat by restrictive pruning.

Russian-olive has a narrow gray leaf much like that of the true olive. The two trees are not related. The Russian-olive withstands either the cold and dryness of the Great Plains or the moist salt air of seaside gardens.

The gray foliage of the Russian-olive is a good foil for bright flowers and for colored foliage plants. (*Roche*)

Columnar, Pendulous, and Colored-foliage Trees
Listed According to Hardiness [1]

See Zones of Hardiness Map (frontispiece).
(*) Better adapted to southern sector of zone.

Hardiness Zone 3: −40 to −30 degrees: Columnar White Birch, Cutleaf European Birch, Columnar Siberian Crab-apple, Sargent Weeping Hemlock, Scanlon Maple, Wilson Columnar Mountain-ash, Russian-olive, Colorado Blue Spruce.

Hardiness Zone 4: −30 to −20 degrees: Red Jade Crab-apple, Sunburst Honey-locust, Columnar Sugar Maple, Crimson King Maple, Erect Norway Maple, Fassens Black Maple, Globe Norway Maple, Lombardy Poplar.

Hardiness Zone 5: −30 to −10 degrees: Copper Beech, Dawyck Beech, Weeping Beech, Welch Flowering Dogwood, Camperdown Elm, Columnar Hawthorn, Pyramidal European Hornbeam, Thundercloud Plum, Weeping Willow, Contorted Hankow Willow.

Hardiness Zone 6: −10 to 0 degrees: Amanogawa Flowering Cherry(*), Columnar Sargent Cherry, Weeping Japanese Cherry(*), Bloodleaf Japanese Maple, Pyramidal English Oak.

Hardiness Zone 7: 0 to 10 degrees: Blue Atlas Cedar.

[1] For descriptions, cultural notes, and botanical names of these trees, see Chapter 15.

CHAPTER 11

A Dozen Fast-growing Trees

As we have seen, rapid growth should not be thought of as the mark of a good plant; after all, the weeds that grow faster than flowers don't have a very good reputation.

There are fast-growing trees, but before we plant any of them, let us review their debits.

Fast-growing trees do not develop strong fibers, so that stormy weather, be it sleet, wet snow, or heavy winds, takes its toll. Wood-rotting fungi that enter through scars in the trunk work more rapidly in such a tree than in the slower-growing species. Large limbs may fall and do great damage to property or passerby. These trees are too short lived to occupy valuable space. They can crowd out or ruin the shape of more desirable specimens that have a longer life expectancy. Their root systems are shallow and vigorous; they are notorious for clogging drain pipes, breaking sidewalks and curbs. They have more than their share of serious pests and often the trees don't warrant the cost of control measures.

Yet I know there is a time and a place for the fast-growing tree. It provides shade more quickly, and shade and the mellowing effect of large trees are often sorely needed.

If, then, it seems necessary to plant a fast-growing tree, plant a tree of better quality at the same time, but try to keep these separated by at least 40 feet. Remember that the fast-growing specimen should be removed *after 20 years*. It will have served its purpose while the better one was becoming established; furthermore, after this length of time it will be a liability—and increasingly expensive to remove as it grows larger.

Rapid Growers

Weeping willow has been and still remains a favorite of home owners. It definitely is of rapid growth. It is inexpensive; in fact, you can start one with a rooted twig from a friend's tree. It leafs out so early that it is a better prophet of spring than the first robins. Watching the twigs turn a spring-like yellow against a fresh blue sky and looking for the first green fuzziness of leaves may be as exciting as bird watching. The willow grows well in some places while in others its life is shortened by cankers on trunk and stem and by other assorted ailments.

Carolina and Lombardy poplars were widely planted several decades ago. Since time, abetted by various diseases, has taken its toll, many of the older plantings have disappeared. Carolina poplar is not looked upon with favor today, and many communities have ordinances forbidding its use along city streets. People continue to plant the Lombardy poplar as a screen even though we now have better columnar trees to choose from.

Japanese poplar is not well known although it may be the best of the lot. It has a dark, glossy leaf much thicker than that of other poplars.

The red maple has a higher rating than other trees discussed in this chapter. In the summer its leaves are a normal green but when the autumn season arrives it is among the first to show color, generally a bright red. Its springtime flowers are redder than those of other large maples.

The Scanlon maple is a select form of the red maple. Its narrow conical shape makes it a desirable tree where the normal, wide-spreading type would crowd or give excessive shade in restricted areas.

Silver maple was once thought of as being *the* tree to plant. It was a maple and it gave quick results. Many a street was lined with this tree, and the result has been no end of trouble.

Gray birch has a white trunk and is commonly seen as a multistemmed tree. Its leaves are small; side branches are slender; and its trunk is never large—all of which gives an open, graceful effect.

Catalpa is coarse of foliage and in winter gives a rather barren appearance since it has no small twigs. It is redeemed by showy white flowers in late June, an off-season for flowering trees.

Chinese elm and "Chinese" elm are not the same. A tree that

is well known and sold as the "Chinese" is actually the Siberian elm. The true Chinese elm is rarely seen.

The widely planted Siberian elm is a very fast grower. The limbs are readily broken by storms, but it does send out replacement branches. It fares better in the dry Plains States than it does in the East with its heavier rainfall.

The true Chinese elm flowers in the fall, while the Siberian is spring flowering. In neither instance is the flower showy. The Chinese elm does not grow quite as rapidly as the Siberian but it is less subject to storm damage. It has small, dark green leaves which are held late in the fall.

Several plants discussed under "Large Shade Trees" (Chapter 8) grow quite rapidly and are more highly regarded than the fast-growing varieties listed here. The chief ones are honey-locust, American elm, and pin oak. Green ash (Chapter 16) might also be included. The pin oak takes a couple of years to become established after transplanting before it starts to grow at an accelerated rate.

Fast-growing Trees Listed According to Hardiness [1]

See Zones of Hardiness Map (frontispiece).
(*) Better adapted to southern sector of zone.

Hardiness Zone 3: –40 to –30 degrees: Siberian Elm(*), Red Maple, Scanlon Maple.

Hardiness Zone 4: –30 to –20 degrees: Silver Maple(*), Carolina Poplar(*), Lombardy Poplar.

Hardiness Zone 5: –20 to –10 degrees: Gray Birch, Western Catalpa, Japanese Poplar, Weeping Willow.

Hardiness Zone 6: –10 to 0 degrees: Chinese Elm.

[1] For descriptions, cultural notes, and botanical names of these trees, see Chapter 15.

CHAPTER 12

Twenty-five Tree-like Shrubs

When we compare some of the small species of trees with mature specimens of large shrubs, we frequently find no clear line of demarcation. About the best distinction we can make is that a tree is a plant that grows to more than 15 feet in height and that generally has a single trunk. A shrub is a plant that is usually less than 15 feet tall and that has many stems arising from the base.

Some of the larger shrubs which grow to more than 15 feet will make very attractive trees if when they attain their full height the lower branches are removed, and if the plant is either trained to a single stem or, better still, grown as a multi-stemmed specimen which will provide a pleasingly informal effect. Training should start after the main stems have reached a diameter of 2 inches. With the lower foliage off, the shrubs lose their massive look; then too, the noteworthy texture and color of the trunk are revealed.

Broad-leaved Evergreens

While very few of the trees within the scope of this book are broad-leaved evergreens, almost half the tree-like shrubs mentioned in this chapter are. Most are for the warmer sections, but three can be used north of New York City.

Rosebay rhododendron with its large leaf and medium-sized white flower is the hardiest. Mountain-laurel, which presents a larger mass of white to pink flowers, is a close second. The fine-textured Japanese holly is third, but every few years its top or even the entire plant is in danger of freezing. Japanese holly resembles boxwood rather than traditional holly because of its small, elliptical leaves; its closely set foliage obscures the berries, which are black.

Farther south, camellia, cherry-laurel, and glossy privet can lend year-round richness to a planting with their large, glossy, dark green leaves. Camellia has the further distinction of beautiful flowers. Cherry-laurel can be pruned to make a hedge. Glossy privet has small clusters of fragrant white flowers followed by blue fruits.

For variation in texture, select the small-leaved tree box, dahoon holly, or yaupon holly which serve well both summer and winter. The two hollies, in contrast to the hardier Japanese species, have red berries.

Osmanthus, known as devilwood, has moderately large evergreen leaves. The flowers, though inconspicuous, give off a pleasant lemon scent.

Colorful Flowers

Three of the shrubs that can be grown as trees produce their flowers when they alone hold center stage. Cornelian-cherry is one of the very earliest of plants to bloom—in small rounded clusters of delicate yellow flowers held close against the stems. Fringe-tree, with its many long narrow white petals, is on display in late spring. Rose-of-Sharon waits for the warmest and driest part of the summer before blooming. Flowers resembling individual hollyhock blossoms cover the plant, and they may be rose to purple, white, or white with a red eye. Of them all, the whites, especially those with a red center, present a fresher appearance at all stages of development. The bluish purples change to poor shades of magenta as they fade.

Returning to spring, we find redvein enkianthus, lilac, and Siberian pea-tree blooming together when the season's floral show is at its peak. The enkianthus puts on another display in autumn, when its leaves become flamboyant in hue—yellow, red, and orange. The Siberian pea-tree has a cheery yellow flower and fine-textured foliage of pale green, unlike anything else in its season.

Showiest of all the flowering tree-like shrubs are camellia and mountain-laurel, mentioned among the broad-leaved evergreens.

Good Foliage

Fine quality of leaf is an essential characteristic of any ornamental plant. As a group, viburnums are noted for their excellent foliage. The nannyberry and blackhaw, two viburnums with treelike propensities, have rich red autumn tones as well as good summer green. A third, the Siebold viburnum, has a deeply veined leaf and an abundance of red berries.

The common buckthorn, with dark green leaves and dull black berries, is one of the hardiest of woody plants. It will grow where conditions are not of the best.

The native American smoke-tree lacks the conspicuous seed and hence the smoky effect that marks the late summer appearance of the more commonly planted European species. It far outshines its relative in autumn, however, when its leaves turn flaming colors.

Chinese quince is virtually unknown, because it is not as showy as the Japanese flowering quince: small pink flowers are mostly hidden by the foliage. But its leathery leaves are superior to those of the Japanese variety, especially since they are long lasting and take on good fall color. When the Chinese shrub is allowed to show its trunk, the smooth peeled surface of greenish tan contrasted with the irregular patches of darker bark is an attractive sight.

Ornamental Berries

The colorful fruits of some shrubs are often longer lasting than the flowers. The dahoon and yaupon hollies and the Siebold viburnum have already been mentioned. The seeds of European spindle-tree, sometimes called "bursting heart," show the relationship to bittersweet; their colors, however, are red and red-purple instead of orange and red.

The orange berries of sea-buckthorn appear in September and contrast brightly with the narrow silvery leaves; they sometimes last until the tiny yellow flowers bloom again in March.

Tree-like Shrubs Listed According to Hardiness [1]

See Zones of Hardiness Map (frontispiece).
(*) Better adapted to southern sector of zone.

Hardiness Zone 2: −50 to −40 degrees: Buckthorn, Siberian Pea-tree.

Hardiness Zone 3: −40 to −30 degrees: Lilac(*), Nannyberry, Sea-buckthorn(*), Blackhaw Viburnum(*).

Hardiness Zone 4: −30 to −20 degrees: Rosebay Rhododendron, European Spindle-tree(*).

Hardiness Zone 5: −20 to −10 degrees: Cornelian-cherry, Redvein Enkianthus, Fringe-tree, Mountain-laurel, Rose-of-Sharon(*), Siebold Viburnum.

Hardiness Zone 6: −10 to 0 degrees: Tree Box, Japanese Holly(*), Chinese Quince, American Smoke-tree.

Hardiness Zone 7: 0 to 10 degrees: Camellia, Cherry-laurel(*), Crape-myrtle, Devilwood, Dahoon Holly(*), Yaupon Holly(*), Glossy Privet(*).

---

[1] For descriptions, cultural notes, and botanical names of these trees, see Chapter 15.

CHAPTER 13

Espalier, Bonsai, Container-grown Trees

Limited space need not rule out the use of trees. For centuries, the Japanese have grown their "little" trees in small pots. With the Japanese, it is a national art, and they hold special shows to display their fine craftsmanship. Bonsai, as their craft is known, is more than the dwarfing of trees. It is the training of a plant to present the rugged, windswept lines of century-old monarchs. If one does not wish to follow the precise training methods of bonsai culture, it is possible to grow trees in large containers and to depend upon pruning alone for the shaping.

Espaliers are plants that are trained flat, in a two-dimensional pattern. They can be used against walls of buildings or fences, or as free-standing hedges or baffles. The espaliers of European tradition were fruit trees, developed into formal patterns. Now, ornamental trees and shrubs are being trained as informal espaliers, a less exacting system and one that is better fitted to our general style of living. Ornamentals require less spraying and have better foliage and a wider range of seasonal interest.

Espalier, bonsai, container-grown trees all lend themselves to the attention of the hobby gardener, and all invite the use of interesting and colorful plants that might not otherwise fit into a garden scheme. They are especially good as finishing touches to terrace or patio. Small- and medium-sized trees are the best subjects, but large trees that would normally grow to 90 feet have been kept to 3 feet when treated as bonsai.

Espaliers

Espaliers offer a fresh approach to a number of landscape planting situations. Foundation plantings are often overdone and appear the same from one house and one street to the next. An espalier in the right place can change an ordinary planting to one of special interest. A narrow planting area or a large barren wall space is an ideal location for an espalier. Flower, leaf, and stem are more clearly delineated; the curved line of branch adds a rhythmic design. A new dimension has been added.

An espaliered plant like this Apple requires only a little space, yet gives distinction to the house. Fruit trees are commonly trained in a formal pattern, while ornamental trees and shrubs are permitted to grow more informally. (*George Taloumis*)

Ornamental trees can rarely be purchased as partially trained espaliers, so you must select plants that show promise for such treatment. A one-sided, open plant is more desirable than a perfectly symmetrical, heavily sheared specimen.

Support—tie—prune: These are the mechanics for developing an espalier. If the plant is to be placed against a masonry wall, copper wire can be used for support. For the espalier that is to be placed against a wooden building, use a wooden frame. Keep the frame 6 to 12 inches away from the building to allow for circulation of air (and to make repainting easier later). Use soft jute cord, rather than wire, for tying: even a plastic-coated wire will cut into the twig as it grows, and the girdling will kill all growth beyond the tie.

Pruning is essential to the development and maintenance of a neatly shaped espalier. If you are not growing a tree for its flowers, you can prune in late winter when the general framework of the plant is more easily studied. But since flower buds of spring-blooming trees are formed the previous summer, these plants should not be pruned until after their flowering season. Prune to maintain a degree of openness so that some of the background surface will show. This enhances the plant itself and contributes to the design. Some slight snipping will be required during early summer to prevent new growth from getting out of bounds.

The espalier pattern may be free-form, informal fan, or, more formally, candelabra or cordon. Free-form emphasizes long, sweeping lines, with an off-center effect. In the informal fan pattern, branches start from a low central trunk and radiate out like the spokes of a wheel. The candelabra is established by training a balanced pair of branches horizontally and then vertically; two, three, or more sets are developed in the same way. The cordon may be either vertical or horizontal, and one or two elongated branches are enough for a simple pattern. Candelabra and cordon designs have long been used in training fruit trees, and they may be used in the training of ornamentals as well.

Since espaliered trees attract an unusual amount of attention, you should choose plants which have more than short seasonal

interest. Good summer foliage should be given prime consideration. Autumn color of leaf adds interest. Floral effects, too, are
important, for they make a vivid impression. Fruits of ornamental
trees can be colorful and long lasting. Stems and a trunk of outstanding structure or color, particularly of older trees, make subtle
contributions.

Deciduous trees that lend themselves to espalier treatment are
Japanese maple, Chinese quince, Japanese dogwood, saucer and
star magnolia, Red Jade crab-apple, Japanese weeping cherry,
Korean stewartia, and blackhaw and Siebold viburnum.

Evergreens, both broad-leaved and needle, are also effective
when espaliered. Camellia, blue Atlas cedar, Japanese holly, southern magnolia, and silver Japanese white pine have been used in
this way.

Bonsai

Dwarfing, shaping, and daily care go into the making of a bonsai.
The dwarfing is accomplished by pruning the branches and roots
as well as by growing the plant in the confined area of a flower pot.
Shaping is done through the use of wires and by pruning. Watering
is the most essential of the daily chores: you will have to syringe
the tops of miniatures in very small pots several times a day during
warm weather.

Specimens of bonsai 1 to 3 feet in height may be as much as a
century or two old, but today's practitioners pride themselves on
making "instant" bonsai by purchasing poorly formed plants and
shaping them with knife and wire. Sometimes native plants are
collected from sterile soil or from a rock ledge. Some of these
plants may have been pruned by browsing animals. (Collection
should not be made without the written permission of the owner,
however.) A gnarled trunk that is large in proportion to the top it
supports is the mark of an aged tree; it adds character to a prize
bonsai.

After a suitable plant has been obtained, a container must be
selected. The Japanese attach a great deal of importance to making

the right choice, and they give it as much thought as an artist gives to the selection of the right frame for a painting. The shallow, dark brown, simply designed containers that come from Japan are hard to improve upon, so bonsai fanciers in this country hunt them out from importers.

In preparation for planting, place a piece of wire mesh or some osmunda fiber over the drainage hole in the pot. Next, cover the bottom of the container with a layer of pebbles. These are aids to drainage, so that water will not remain long enough to damage the roots.

The soil mixture should be one that will drain well. Use two parts of good garden loam and one part each of sharp sand and shredded leafmold or peatmoss. To each bushel of this mixture, add one pint of 5-10-10 fertilizer and the same amount of dried cow manure. Work the soil mixture down between the roots, using a pointed stick.

To water the newly potted plant, place the pot in a tub of water for a few minutes. The water in the tub should come almost to the rim of the pot. Syringe the top of the plant and the soil surface.

A plant is usually placed off-center in the pot. An irregularly shaped plant located in this way gives a pleasing, informal balance. Where there are long, spreading branches on one side, it will be necessary to wire the plant to the container. If there are two drainage holes, as there frequently are in Japanese containers, the process is simple, for the wire can be threaded through both holes (before osmunda fiber, pebbles, and soil are added), over the top of the root system at a point near the trunk, and then fastened. If there is only one hole, a stick or flat metal piece can be placed under the pot to provide an anchor for the wire. Preferably, the wire should be removed after six months, and it certainly should not remain without change for more than a year.

An older plant that has been repotted several times can be somewhat elevated in the pot to expose old roots near the base of the trunk. Since such a condition is found among plants on rocky hillsides, a naturalistic touch is added.

Twisting and shaping of the branches is necessary to the making

Bonsai plants are kept dwarfed and are trained to look old and windswept. Plants in the back row, left to right, are a Larch, a pair of Dwarf Hinoki False-cypresses, and a Pine. A Juniper appears on the terrace. (*George Taloumis*)

of a good bonsai. Use a moderately stiff copper wire and heat it slightly over a moderate flame to improve its bending quality. Beginning at the top, wrap the wire spirally around a branch that is to be shaped, and place the lower end of the wire in the soil near the trunk. You can then bend the branch to the desired shape, although you must be careful not to break it. When wire is to be used on trees with tender bark, such as cherry and maple, it is best to wrap it with rice paper before proceeding. This wire should not remain in place for more than six months because the growing branch will start to expand over it and the girdling will kill, or at least weaken, the branch.

Top-prune to direct the growth of the tree and to keep surplus branches from developing. An open top is desirable so that the trunk will be visible and portions of the principal side branches will show here and there.

Root-pruning is part of the repotting process. Remove two-thirds of the soil. Cut out about one-half of the roots of deciduous plants and no more than a quarter of the roots of the slower-growing evergreens.

Deciduous plants should be repotted every two or three years; evergreens, at intervals of three to five years. This should be done in early spring before new growth starts. Select a place away from sun and wind for this work since exposed roots are easily damaged.

Newly potted plants will not require supplementary fertilizing the first year. Subsequently, mild but weekly applications should be made from early spring until mid-summer, using a soluble fertilizer such as that for house plants, but at half strength.

The hardy plants that are traditionally used for bonsai will not withstand household conditions for any length of time. If you want continuous indoor display, have several plants that can be rotated. In this way, one plant need not remain indoors for more than half a day a week.

In areas where the ground freezes to a depth of several inches, special winter quarters must be provided because if the soil in the containers freezes it will break them. Furthermore, the small quantity of soil in the pot is quickly frozen dry, causing dehydration of the plant. A deep pit covered with a sloping glass frame with a northern exposure is most suitable for storage. Be sure that good drainage is provided and that poison baits are set out to forestall rodent damage.

Trees that grow slowly and those with small leaves or short needles are the best bonsai subjects. Favorite deciduous plants are trident and Japanese maple, hornbeam, Chinese quince, flowering cherry, and zelkova. Among the evergreens are camellia, blue Atlas cedar, cryptomeria, and the several pines, especially the mugo, black, and Japanese white.

Container-grown Trees

Those who do not have the time or the inclination to train and care for bonsai trees should consider a small tree grown in a larger container and trained more casually: it is not nearly so exacting in its requirements. Actually, it need have no more care than that given to a potted geranium.

Terrace and courtyard living increases in popularity every year. Extensive, hard-surfaced areas for automobiles and services are becoming commonplace, with little space left for plantings. Under such circumstances, trees growing in containers provide a happy solution. Geraniums, fuchsias, tuberous begonias, and other flowers in pots can be added to provide color. They combine nicely with the taller potted trees. Any plant in a container is set off as an individual, thereby gaining new importance.

Potted trees serve as excellent accents for an entrance. They can also be placed in such a way as to provide background for terrace furniture or a frame for a piece of sculpture. Since these plants are movable, different groupings can be arranged as the seasons change, or, if you tire of a plant, you can move it to some out-of-the-way place.

A large clay pot, or a tub or box, preferably made of redwood or cedar for long-lasting qualities, is necessary for a tree. A 6- to 8-foot plant needs a container that is 15 to 20 inches deep. A low evergreen, spreading to 3 feet in width, will do well in a pot that is 12 inches in diameter and 7 inches deep.

The potting mixture should consist of two parts of good garden loam to one part each of sharp sand and shredded leafmold or peatmoss. To each bushel of the soil mix, add one pint of 5-10-10 fertilizer and one quart of dried cow manure. Do not fill the container to the rim; allow an ample basin to hold water. A basin 2 inches deep is desirable for large receptacles.

Water every day or two, or whenever the top layer of soil becomes dry. If you are to be away for several days, give the plants a double watering. Apply the regular amount of water six to ten hours before you expect to leave; then, just before leaving, water again.

Daily watering and heavy rainfalls leach out nutrients from the soil in containers, especially small containers. Yellowing of the leaves and a slowdown in flower bud formation are indications that the plant needs fertilizing. Supplementary feeding will not be necessary during the first month after potting, but thereafter apply a liquid fertilizer every two weeks until mid-summer. Use a soluble, house-plant fertilizer, mixing it with water at half the strength recommended for flowering plants.

When ground-freezing season arrives, steps need to be taken to provide winter protection. The plant should be removed from the pot. If it were to remain, the frost action would break the container, or the soil would lose its moisture during the freezing process and the plant would suffer. Since a network of roots will have formed near the sides of the container, the plant can quite easily be pulled out of the receptacle. It can then be planted out in a vegetable or cutting garden, to remain until the following spring. After the ground has frozen, mulch around the tree with leafmold to give some protection against deep freezing of the soil and against alternate thawing and freezing.

In the spring, move the plant in a wheelbarrow to the terrace where the potting can be done. At that time the old soil mass should be reduced and the roots pruned. Cut out about half the roots of deciduous plants and no more than a quarter of the roots of evergreens. Then pot the tree, using a fresh supply of soil mix.

If the containers are larger than usual and if they are made of reinforced concrete or heavy boards, the more hardy deciduous trees can remain in them. Amur maple, ginkgo, crab-apple, and contorted Hankow willow will withstand sub-zero weather. Where

The pendulous branches of Red Jade Crab-apple provide a pleasing silhouette. When the tree is grown in a container, the pattern is emphasized. In
late autumn, numerous small red fruits add a jewel-like quality. (*Brooklyn
Botanic Garden*)

winters are not severe, south of New York City, broad-leaved and
needle evergreens can also stay in large containers throughout the
year. Be sure that the plants are well watered before the ground
freezes; then water during mild, snowless periods through the
winter. After the ground freezes, mulch the soil with a 3-inch layer
of shredded pine bark mixed with peatmoss.

Some deciduous plants that are attractive when grown in containers are Japanese maple, ginkgo, goldenchain, crape-myrtle,
star and saucer magnolia, Red Jade crab-apple, Hankow contorted
willow, and ringleaf willow.

A number of evergreens have been successfully used. Camellia,
blue Atlas cedar, Japanese and American holly, glossy privet,
southern magnolia, Japanese white and black pine, and umbrella-
pine have outstanding qualities that appear to advantage in clay
pot or wooden tub.

CHAPTER 14

Fruit and Nut Trees

Great satisfaction can be derived from fruits and nuts that are grown at home. However, since their care and placement present problems, you should not start with either kind of tree before you are aware of the many varied routines that must precede the harvesting of an edible crop.

Fruit Trees

Although a home orchard cannot be expected to reduce the family's expenditure for food, it can furnish fruits of good quality and of varieties not available in the market. But to obtain these you must spray your trees no less than five times a year to keep the fruit free from pests; seven applications will assure a better crop. (The commercial grower sprays 15 to 20 times a year.)

Furthermore, the trees must be protected from ravages by rabbits, mice, and birds. Rabbits chew the bark in winter; keep them at bay with a cylinder of quarter-inch mesh wire. Mice girdle trunk and roots at or just below ground level; use poison baits for them. Birds like fruit, especially cherries, even before they are ripe; cover these trees with a netting in advance of their raids.

Wherever fruit trees are planted, they need an open area so that larger trees will not interfere with their growth. Also, they must have fertile soil on a well-drained site. Good air drainage is desirable, for in a frost pocket—a low place from which cold air cannot escape—late spring cold may damage opening flowers.

Ample spacing between trees is required, so that the sun can reach developing fruit. Peaches, plums, and dwarf pears need to be 20 feet apart; apples grafted on Malling #9 dwarfing stock should be 10 to 15 feet apart.

Malling #9 will result in a tree not more than 10 feet tall, and so its fruits can be easily harvested. This dwarf tree needs staking because of the brittle root system of this stock.

To develop a dwarf pear, it is best to graft onto quince. Peaches, nectarines, and plums do best when grafted onto the western sand cherry (*Prunus besseyi*) or the Manchu cherry (*Prunus tomentosa*). Cherries themselves do not dwarf satisfactorily.

To achieve a good set of fruit, bees must be present at blossom time—a neighbor's if not your own. You should also have at least two varieties of any one fruit, so that cross-pollination can take place.

Varieties of fruit, spray schedules, and pruning and other practices vary from one part of the country to another. Bulletins on these aspects have been prepared by State Agricultural Extension Services and Experiment Stations, and they are available from local County Agricultural Agents as well as directly from the institutions.

Nut Trees

Nut trees require space, for they grow large. They should be planted by themselves so that falling nuts will not interfere with lawn-mowing, passersby, or traffic.

The use of seedling nut trees is not recommended. It is far better to purchase small-size grafted plants of the newer named varieties from a nursery that specializes in nut trees. Plant two named varieties of the same species near each other to insure proper cross-pollination. Most nuts bear good crops only every second year.

Many nut trees are sensitive to weather—late spring or early autumn frosts or severe winter temperatures. Learn the needs and weaknesses of the trees you want before you plant them.

Here are some kinds to try:

Butternut (*Juglans cinerea*) is hardy and does not require a rich soil. It is shorter lived than most nut trees. Selected strains are Buckley, Craxezy, and Wescheke.

Chestnut, Chinese (*Castanea mollissima*) is commonly produced from seed. At maturity it is no larger than an apple tree. It is fairly hardy. More than one tree must be present for proper cross-pollination.

Heartnut (*Juglans cordiformis*), a kind of walnut which has a good cracking quality, generally grows no larger than an apple tree. Temperatures of 20 degrees below zero are likely to kill it. Bates, Gellatly, and Walters are recommended varieties.

Hickory, Shagbark (*Carya ovata*) is the hardiest of the edible nut trees. Fairbanks, Lingenfelter, Schinnerling, and Shaul are improved varieties with nuts that are easier to crack than are those of native seedlings.

Hickory, Shellbark (*Carya laciniosa*), sometimes called kingnut, bears a larger nut than the shagbark hickory but is not as hardy. It can, however, be grown through most of Pennsylvania and into southern New England. It likes a rich, lowland site, and will withstand wetter soil than the shagbark will.

Pecan (*Carya pecan*) is traditionally associated with the cotton-belt area and is common into southern Illinois and Indiana. Varieties for those areas are Bradley, Brooks, Curtis, and Stuart. Considerable testing has gone into the search for more hardy strains, the best of which so far are Greenriver, Major, and Posey.

Walnut, Black (*Juglans nigra*) requires a rich loamy soil and grows best where it is not acid. Myers, Ohio, Stabler, and Thomas are some of the better selections.

Walnut, English or Persian (*Juglans regia*) has been tried over a wide area. Winter temperatures that reach 20 degrees below zero generally kill this tree. The Carpathian walnut is a hardy strain that has survived temperatures of 40 degrees below zero. Named varieties are Hansen, McKinster, and Metcalf.

PART THREE
Descriptive Lists and Landscape Uses

CHAPTER 15

Select Trees Described

My purpose has been to select a limited number of trees for their good qualities of leaf, flower, and stem; their good form; their adaptability to growth and survival in man-made settings; and their appropriateness for use in a variety of landscape situations. A few trees have been included, not on their general merits, but because they meet some special need. In such instances, their shortcomings as well as their good points have been mentioned.

Major plants described in this chapter have been included in the discussions in Chapters 6 through 13, and plant lists appear in Chapter 17.

Height and Flowering Period

The height given is that which may reasonably be expected of the plant as it grows under *suburban* conditions where it must compete with lawns and paved areas. Many of these plants would grow considerably taller under woodland conditions in their native habitats.

The flowering dates used are from the records of Dr. Donald Wyman of the Arnold Arboretum near Boston. Plants that blossom in that vicinity during mid-May would flower in the New York City area in early May. The opening date advances as one goes south, so that for northern Florida there would be a difference of two months.

Zones of Hardiness

The map showing the zones of plant hardiness which appears as the frontispiece was prepared in 1960 by the United States Department of Agriculture and the National Arboretum cooperating with

109

the American Horticultural Society. This map shows a more detailed division of area than did the 1948 USDA map. Since the older map has been widely used, I want to emphasize that zones 4, 5, and 6 are markedly different on the two maps. The plants described here are keyed to the 1960 map.

On large colored copies of the 1960 map, each zone is further divided into *a* and *b* sectors representing a 5-degree change in temperature in contrast to the 10-degree change between zones. For simplicity, the subdivisions indicating *a* and *b* sectors have not been included on the reduced map in this book. However, in the descriptions, some plants carry an asterisk after the zone number. This indicates that these plants are better adapted to the southern sector of the zone.

The approximate range of the average annual minimum temperatures for each zone is:

Zone 2	−50 to	−40 degrees
Zone 3	−40 to	−30 degrees
Zone 4	−30 to	−20 degrees
Zone 5	−20 to	−10 degrees
Zone 6	−10 to	0 degrees
Zone 7	0 to	10 degrees

Arborvitae, American (*Thuja occidentalis*). Needle evergreen. Broadly columnar. Rate of growth, moderately rapid. Zone 3.

Height.   40 to 50 feet.

Leaf.   Flat, overlapping foliage of medium coarse texture is appressed to the branches. Bright green when growing well; yellowish green on poor sites.

Culture.   Deep porous soil with ample moisture; prefers a humid atmosphere. The top should be kept narrow and not allowed to develop height too quickly; otherwise, wet, heavy snows may deform the plant.

Habitat.   Southern Canada, the Lake States, the Northeast, and the Appalachian Mountains.

Uses.   Tall screen. Requires little pruning.

Comment.   Its density, rather rapid growth, and relative inexpensiveness combine to make this plant popular. Takes on a yellowish brown cast during winter months. Horticultural selections such as Dark American Arborvitae (*Thuja occidentalis nigra*) retain good color throughout the winter and keep to a lower height—about 30 feet.

Pyramidal Arborvitae (*Thuja occidentalis pyramidalis*) is a narrowly columnar tree. Height about 30 feet. Zone 3.

Beech, American (*Fagus grandifolia*). Deciduous. Round-topped, with spreading, horizontal branches. Moderately dense, becoming open with age. Rate of growth, slow. Zone 4*.

Height. 80 feet.

Leaf and Bark. Leaves are 2 to 4 inches long and ¾ to 2½ inches wide; bright green, turning a rich brown in autumn. Trunk is light gray and smooth.

Culture. Sandy loam. Start with small plants, for tree is very difficult to transplant.

Habitat. Eastern North America.

Uses. At edge of woods. Trunk is very effective when seen against evergreens.

Comment. The trunk is a lighter gray than that of the European species. Also, the tree is less dense and more likely to lose its lower branches. Not commonly sold. Formerly known as *Fagus americana*.

Beech, European (*Fagus sylvatica*). Deciduous. Tends to retain wide-spreading branches to the ground. Very dense. Rate of growth, slow. Zone 5.

Height. 80 feet.

Leaf and Bark. Leaves are 2 to 3½ inches long, 1½ to 2½ inches wide; bright green, quite glossy, and of medium texture. They turn to an attractive golden brown in the autumn and are held late. Bark is a darker gray than that of the American species.

Culture. Prefers rich, light loam. Has many surface roots and cannot withstand compaction of the soil or even a moderate amount of extra soil placed over the established grade. Difficult to move in larger sizes. Not as hardy as the American beech but does better under cultivation and is therefore more readily available in the trade.

Habitat. Central and southern Europe to the Crimea. Has long been in cultivation.

Uses. As a lawn specimen, especially such selections as copper and fernleaf beech.

Comment. It is wide spreading and throws heavy shade, therefore it is best for spacious grounds. Noted for its smooth gray bark. Numerous horticultural clones are highly esteemed. Among them are:

Copper Beech (*Fagus sylvatica atropunicea*). Height, 70 feet. Zone 5.

Rivers Beech (*F. s.* 'Rivers'). Foliage is a deeper color than that of copper beech. Height, 70 feet. Zone 5.

Dawyck Beech (*F. s. fastigiata*). Height, 60 feet. Zone 5.

Weeping Beech (*F. s. pendula*). Height, 60 feet. Zone 5.

Fernleaf Beech (*F. s. asplenifolia*). Height, 60 feet. Zone 5.

Tricolor Beech (*F. s.* 'Tricolor'). Height, 60 feet. Zone 5.

Birch, Columnar White (*Betula pendula fastigiata*). Deciduous. Narrow, columnar, becoming somewhat broader at the top. Side branches parallel main trunk. Rate of growth, moderately rapid. Zone 3.

Height.   50 feet.

Leaf and Bark.   Leaf is 2½ to 3½ inches long, 1½ to 2½ inches wide, broad at base, long tapering, dark bright green. Holds color late, then turns yellow before dropping. Trunk and larger branches are white.

Culture.   Tolerant, but responds to good, well-drained soil. Needs light to develop a well-branched plant. Withstands city conditions. Bronze birch borer may be troublesome.

Habitat.   Europe, Asia Minor.

Uses.   Lawn specimen. Screen.

Comment.   One of the better columnar trees. The white trunk provides winter interest.

Cutleaf European Birch (*Betula pendula gracilis*) is widely planted. It is a graceful tree with its smaller leaves and thin pendulous branches. Height, 50 feet. Zone 3.

European White Birch (*Betula pendula*), the species from which these forms are derived, is a wide-spreading tree with a white trunk but without the peeling bark of the native American paper birch. This was formerly known as *Betula alba* and *Betula verrucosa*. Height, 60 feet. Zone 3.

Birch, Gray (*Betula populifolia*). Deciduous. Irregularly upright, generally multi-stemmed. Small side branches. Open. Rate of growth, rapid. Zone 5.

Height.   30 to 40 feet.

Leaf and Bark.   Leaf is triangular with long slender point, 2 to 3½ inches long, 1½ to 2½ inches wide; medium light green turning to yellow in autumn. Trunk varies from gray-white to white, with dark triangular marks below side branches. Bark does not peel except in some natural hybrids with paper birch.

Culture.   Will grow on the poorest of soils and with little moisture. Fibrous roots; easily moved. Spring planting is recommended. Leaf miner is troublesome.

Habitat.   Northeastern North America.

Uses.   Lawns, where an upright tree giving light shade is desired. The line effect provided by a grove of multiple white stems is attractive.

Comments.   With its slender, short side branches and the comparatively small size of its trunks, it provides an open, airy effect not found in any other tree. Tall specimens may be bent almost to the ground by sleet storms, but surprisingly they will straighten up again time after time. They are more subject to this bending than are other birches. Short lived. Sometimes called Old-field Birch or Poplar Birch.

Birch, Paper (*Betula papyrifera*). Deciduous. Spreading, with open top. White trunk carries the eye upward. Slender branches are moderately pendulous. Rate of growth, moderate. Zone 2.

Height. 65 feet.

Leaf and Bark. Leaf is 1½ to 3½ inches long and two-thirds as wide; yellow-green at first, becoming a medium green, then turning to yellow or yellow-orange in the autumn. Trunk and secondary branches of older specimens are pure white and are covered with a chalklike substance. Bark peels in paper-thin sections.

Culture. Moist loam with ample humus, well drained. Good fibrous root system, therefore easily transplanted. Spring planting is recommended. Leaf miner is troublesome unless sprayed twice a year.

Habitat. Maine to Washington, much of Canada.

Uses. Lawn specimen. A grove on a hillside or against an evergreen planting is most effective. Multi-stemmed specimens are prized.

Comment. Prefers the cooler summers of the North. Farther south, other white-barked birches such as gray birch and European white birch may be used. No other tree has the same degree of whiteness as the paper birch. May be known as Canoe Birch or White Birch. The State tree of New Hampshire.

Birch, White, see **Birch, Paper.**

Blackhaw, see **Viburnum, Blackhaw.**

Box, Tree (*Buxus sempervirens arborescens*). Broad-leaved evergreen shrub; older specimens may attain stature of a small tree. Loose-growing plant of irregular outline unless sheared. Rate of growth, rapid. Zone 6.

Height. 25 feet.

Leaf. Small, narrow leaf, medium dark green. Foliage has a characteristic musky scent which is more noticeable on muggy days.

Culture. Good garden soil that is well drained; either acid or alkaline. It is the least compact member of the Box clan, therefore requires regular pruning to maintain a shapely plant. A mulch helps to protect this shallow-rooted plant. Leaf miners may attack.

Habitat. Southern Europe, northern Africa, western Asia.

Uses. Tall screen; or where one desires a tall, broad-leaved evergreen that is loose growing and of medium fine texture.

Comment. If not pruned regularly to maintain some degree of compactness it will become topheavy and shapeless.

Buckthorn (*Rhamnus cathartica*). Deciduous shrub; older specimens may attain stature of a small tree. Round-headed, wider than it is high. Rate of growth, moderate. Zone 2.

Height. 20 feet.

Leaf, Flower, Fruit. Dark green leaf, which is held late without change of color; 1 to 2 inches long and half as wide. Flowers are small, green, insignificant. Black fruit in clusters; single fruit is ¼ inch across; held through much of the winter. No spines as in other buck-thorns, but there is a small spur-like growth between the terminal leaflets.

Culture. Tolerant of a variety of soil conditions. Fibrous rooted; easily transplanted. Withstands city conditions.

Habitat. Europe, western and northern Asia. Has been in cul-tivation for centuries.

Uses. As a screen at rear of property; or to hide unsightly walls.

Comment. One of the most hardy of plants and remarkably free of pests. Fruit clusters are attractive in the winter. Retains lower branches unless they are removed to make a tree-like plant.

Bull Bay, see **Magnolia, Southern.**

Bursting Heart, see **Spindle-tree, European.**

Buttonball, see **Plane, London.**

Camellia (*Camellia japonica*). Broad-leaved evergreen shrub; older specimens may attain stature of a small tree. Broadly oval in shape. Rate of growth, slow. Zone 7.

Height. 20 feet.

Leaf and Flower. Dark green leaf is glossy and leathery, 3 to 4 inches long, oval. The red, pink, or white flowers are very showy; many named varieties, some of which are fully double while others are semi-double or single. Blooms in the winter or early spring.

Culture. Prefers partially shaded location; should not be exposed to winter sun or strong winds. Light, semi-acid, well-drained soil. Feed lightly with an azalea or holly fertilizer at end of flowering period.

Habitat. China and Japan.

Uses. Lawn specimen or as a background for a garden. Good as an espalier.

Comment. The showy flowers and the excellent foliage help to make this a choice plant. Hardier clones are now being tried in the Philadelphia area. In general, late-blooming varieties are proving to be hardier than early types.

Camellia, False, see **Stewartia, Korean.**

Catalpa, Western (*Catalpa speciosa*). Deciduous. Irregular in shape; very broad, oval. Open. Rate of growth, rapid. Zone 5.
Height. 50 to 60 feet.
Leaf and Flower. Leaves are 5 to 12 inches long, 3 to 8 inches wide, heart shaped; light green. Flowers, 2 inches in diameter, and white with yellowish markings, are in upright, 6-inch clusters. Blooms late in June. Seed is slender, beanlike pod, up to 18 inches long.
Culture. Tolerant, but does best in well-drained, moist soil. Transplants readily.
Habitat. Indiana to northern Arkansas.
Uses. Temporary lawn tree for large properties.
Comments. Coarse in summer foliage and winter twigs. Very late to leaf out in spring. Flower is attractive and appears in an off-season.
Umbrella Catalpa (*Catalpa bignonioides nana*) is a dwarf nonflowering tree that must be pruned severely every winter. Although it was once widely planted, because of its coarseness and formality it is out of style today.

Cedar, Blue Atlas (*Cedrus atlantica glauca*). Needle evergreen. Broad, conical, becoming flat-topped with age; lower branches are horizontal and wide spreading. Rate of growth, moderate. Zone 7.
Height. 80 feet.
Leaf and Cone. Pale blue-green needles, ½ inch long; numerous, in a cluster, appearing on short spurs in the same manner as the larch. Decorative cones are 3 inches long and upright.
Culture. Good garden soil, well drained. Move with a ball of soil in the spring.
Habitat. North Africa.
Uses. Lawn specimen.
Comment. Distinctive in color and needle arrangement. This is one of the few true cedars and is not to be confused with red-cedar, which is a juniper.

Cherry, Amanogawa Flowering (*Prunus serrulata* 'Amanogawa'). Deciduous. Columnar. Rate of growth, moderate. Zone 6*.
Height. 20 feet.
Leaf and Flower. Leaf is medium light green, 4 to 5 inches long and half as wide; yellow to red in autumn. Flowers are light pink, semi-double, 1¾ inches in diameter. Blooms in mid-May. Rarely sets fruit.

Culture.   Good soil, ample moisture. Borers may attack the trunk.
Habitat.   Japan.
Uses.   Near corner of house. As an accent in the garden.
Comment.   One of the few columnar trees noted for its flowers; also this one has the distinction of being of restricted size.

Cherry, Kwanzan Flowering (*Prunus serrulata* 'Kwanzan'). Deciduous. Irregularly round-headed. Rate of growth, moderate. Zone 6*.
Height.   20 to 25 feet.
Leaf and Flower.   Leaves are 3 to 5 inches long, 1¼ to 2½ inches wide, medium dark green. Flowers are semi-double, deep bluish pink, 1½ inches wide. Blooms in mid-May.
Culture.   Tolerant. Responds to good, well-drained soil. Borers may be troublesome.
Habitat.   Species is native to Japan, China, and Korea, and has been cultivated in Japan for centuries.
Uses.   Lawn or garden specimen.
Comment.   The most widely planted of the many named varieties of flowering cherry. The large semi-double flower has appeal, though the bluish pink color is not admired by everyone.
Other varieties to choose from are:
Yedo Cherry (*Prunus serrulata* 'Yedo Zakura'), pale pink to white. Height, 20 to 25 feet. Zone 6*.
Hokusai Cherry (*Prunus serrulata* 'Hokusai'), pink with a tint of orange. Height, 20 to 25 feet. Zone 6*.
Mt. Fuji Cherry (*Prunus serrulata* 'Mt. Fuji'), double and white. Height, 20 to 25 feet. Zone 6*.

Cherry, Sargent (*Prunus sargenti*). Deciduous. Round-headed. Dense. Rate of growth, moderate. Zone 6.
Height.   50 feet.
Leaf and Flower.   Leaves are 3 to 5 inches long and about half as wide; medium green, turning to yellow-orange in autumn. The pink flowers open in late April.
Culture.   Good garden soil, well drained. Advisable to move it with a ball of soil. Borers may be troublesome.
Habitat.   Japan.
Uses.   Lawn or garden specimen.
Comment.   Most hardy and vigorous of Japanese cherries. Single flowers which are followed by bronzy red young leaves offer early season color. Autumn color is outstanding. A tree of medium size that might well be used more frequently.
Columnar Sargent Cherry (*Prunus sargenti columnaris*) is one of

the few columnar trees that is noted for flowers. They are pink and open in late April. Height, 35 feet. Zone 6.

Rancho® Columnar Sargent Cherry (*Prunus sargenti columnaris* 'Rancho') (Plant Patent 2065) is a selected clone that is of especially good shape.

Cherry, Weeping Japanese (*Prunus subhirtella pendula*). Deciduous. Round-topped with pendulous branches. Rate of growth, moderate. Zone 6*.

Height. 30 feet.

Leaf and Flower. Leaves are medium dark green, 3 inches long and half as wide. Flowers are light pink, single; late April.

Culture. Good soil preferred. Provide adequate moisture. Borers in trunk may be troublesome.

Habitat. Japan.

Uses. Lawn specimen. Espalier.

Comment. The most widely admired of pendulous trees. There is a double-flowered form as well as one with deep pink flowers.

Cherry-laurel (*Prunus laurocerasus*). Broad-leaved evergreen shrub; older specimens may attain stature of a small tree. Wide-spreading. Rate of growth, rapid. Zone 7*.

Height. 15 to 18 feet.

Leaf, Flower, Fruit. Leaves are 4 to 6 inches long; very glossy dark green, thick and leathery. White flowers in 2- to 5-inch racemes, in late May, are followed by purple-black fruits of less than ½-inch diameter.

Culture. Good soil. Should not be permitted to dry out. Needs protection from winter winds in its northern limits. Because it is a heavy feeder, its use near a flower or vegetable garden is inadvisable.

Habitat. Southeastern Europe, Asia Minor.

Uses. Screen. Popular as a hedge in the South.

Comment. The leaf resembles that of the true laurel (*Laurus nobilis*) of Greece. Sometimes called English-laurel. Formerly listed as *Laurocerasus officinalis*.

Of the numerous horticultural forms, *Prunus laurocerasus schipkaensis* is one of the most common, also the most hardy, specimen plants, having been grown as far north as Rochester, New York, when given some protection. Height, 15 to 18 feet. Zone 7*.

Chittam-wood, see **Smoke-tree, American.**

Cork-tree, Amur (*Phellodendron amurense*). Deciduous. Spreading, rounded. Quite open. Rate of growth, rapid in early years. Zone 3*.

Height. 45 feet.

Leaf, Flower, Fruit, Bark. Compound leaf, 10 to 15 inches long, with 5 to 11 leaflets each of which is 2 to 4½ inches long; dark green. Late to leaf out in the spring, but holds leaves late in the fall with little change of color. Male and female flowers are on separate plants. Flower in early June is not conspicuous. Clusters of black berries, each ½ inch in diameter, persist for several months. Bark of mature tree is very spongy, light colored, and deeply fissured.

Culture. Tolerant of a variety of soils. Withstands city conditions and drought. Fibrous roots, therefore transplants readily. Few pests.

Habitat. Northern China, Manchuria.

Uses. Lawn specimen. Street tree; use male clones since fruit might prove to be a nuisance.

Comment. Looks like a small, dark-leaved ash but is more pest-free and withstands poorer growing conditions. Since its shade is not dense this tree does not compete with lawns.

Cornelian-cherry (*Cornus mas*). Deciduous shrub; older specimens may attain stature of a small tree. Round-headed; quite dense. Normally retains lower branches which sweep the ground. Rate of growth, moderately rapid. Zone 5.

Height. 15 to 20 feet.

Leaf, Flower, Fruit. Leaves are generally rounded, 2 inches long and 1½ inches wide; dark green with little or no fall color; medium texture. Foliage is held late. Small pale yellow flowers open in early April. Bright red fruit resembles a large elongated cherry and ripens in late summer; sour but edible.

Culture. Prefers rich, well-drained soil. Will grow in partial shade but is more compact when in full sun. Young plants are easily transplanted. Pests are rarely troublesome.

Habitat. Central and southern Europe, western Asia. It has been cultivated since ancient times and was used in Colonial gardens.

Uses. In a garden for early spring display. Flowering stems are very effective against a red building.

Comment. The yellow flowers precede those of forsythia. The dark green foliage is an asset.

Japanese Cornelian-cherry (*Cornus officinalis*) has larger flowers in more sizable clusters and it blossoms somewhat earlier in the season. Height, 15 to 20 feet. Zone 5.

Crab-apple, Flowering (*Malus*). Deciduous. Broad, round-topped. Rate of growth, moderately rapid. Zone 4, except as noted.

Height.   25 feet, except as noted.

Leaf, Flower, Fruit.   Leaves are 2½ to 3 inches long, 1½ inches wide; medium green. Flowers may be white, pink, red, or a purplish red, and either single or double. Blooms in mid-May, except as noted. Fruits are generally red or yellow, varying in size from less than ½ inch to 1 inch.

Culture.   Tolerant of a variety of soil and moisture conditions. Easily transplanted. Blossoms a year or two after moving. Few pests, unlike the common apple.

Habitat.   Japan; or of garden origin.

Uses.   To give height to a shrub border or as an intermediate plant between shade trees and shrubs. Combine crab-apples of contrasting colors to intensify floral effect.

Comment.   Large masses of blossoms extend from the tips of the twigs almost to the center of the tree. The small fruits do not require spraying or raking. Will flourish where other trees have difficulty in becoming established.

There are many varieties of fine crab-apples. In a number of particulars they are similar although they do vary in flower color and, to a lesser degree, in fruit color and size. The following have been chosen to provide a diversity of floral effects as well as variation in height and habit.

Variety	Flower	Fruit	Comments
Arnold Crab-apple (*Malus arnoldiana*)	Pink to white	Yellow	Very floriferous.
Bechtel Crab-apple (*Malus ioensis plena*)	Pink	Green	Double, fragrant. Late May. Cedar rust is troublesome.
Columnar Siberian Crab-apple (*Malus baccata columnaris*)	White	Yellow	The most columnar. Height, 35 feet. Zone 3. Early May. Street tree.
Dorothea Crab-apple (*Malus* 'Dorothea')	Pink	Yellow	Semi-double; abundance of showy fruit, which is held late.
Hopa Crab-apple (*Malus* 'Hopa')	Purplish pink	Red	Fruit is ¾ inch in diameter. Street tree.
Japanese Flowering Crab-apple (*Malus floribunda*)	Pink to white	Yellow with red cheek	Deep red buds open pink, turn to white.
Jay Darling Crab-apple (*Malus* 'Jay Darling')	Purplish red	Deep red	One-inch fruit, dark red to the core.
Katherine Crab-apple (*Malus* 'Katherine')	Pink to white	Yellow	Double, delicate pink flower. Street tree.
Redbud Crab-apple (*Malus zumi calocarpa*)	Pink to white	Red	Noted for fruit, which is held late.

Variety	Flower	Fruit	Comments
Red Jade Crab-apple (*Malus* 'Red Jade') (Plant Patent 1497)	White	Red	Quantities of small red fruits held late on pendulous branches.
Sargent Crab-apple (*Malus sargenti*)	White	Red	The most dwarf: 6 to 8 feet.
Siberian Crab-apple (*Malus baccata*)	White	Red	The tallest: 50 feet. Zone 3. Early May. Street tree.
Tea Crab-apple (*Malus hupehensis*)	Pink to white	Yellow to red	Picturesque branching habit.

Crape-myrtle (*Lagerstroemia indica*). Deciduous shrub; older specimens may attain stature of a small tree. Upright with irregularly rounded top, often multi-stemmed. Open. Rate of growth, moderate. Zone 7.

Height.   20 feet.

Leaf, Flower, Bark.   Leaves are 1 to 2½ inches long and a little more than half as wide. Flowers, each 1 to 1½ inches wide, deep pink and crinkled, are arranged in clusters to 8 inches long and 5 inches wide. There is a long flowering period during the summer. Trunk and older branches are smooth and mottled in shades of gray, tan, and pale green.

Culture.   Clay soil, well drained. Not near the seacoast or where exposed to cold winds. Advisable to cut off old seed heads. Japanese beetles may be troublesome. Mildew disfigures leaves of plants grown in the shade.

Habitat.   China and Korea.

Uses.   Garden or lawn specimen.

Comment.   A favorite garden plant of the South, noted for its long period of bloom and its colorful bark. There are several shades of pink, the bluish pink or magenta flowers being the least desirable.

Cryptomeria (*Cryptomeria japonica*). Needle evergreen. Broad, columnar, dense. Rate of growth, slow. Zone 6*.

Height.   30 to 50 feet.

Leaf and Bark.   Needles are less than ½ inch long, arranged singly and spirally around the twig, even on older wood; blue-green. Older specimens have rounded masses of foliage with open or shadow areas. Reddish brown bark.

Culture.   Light, rich soil with ample moisture. Move with a ball of soil. Protect from cold winds; foliage may turn brownish if exposed to excessive cold. Does well near the seashore. Few pests.

Habitat.   Japan.

Uses.   Lawn specimen. Screen.

Comment. Distinctive appearance. Sometimes called Temple-tree. An ancient temple in Japan has for an approach a double row of cryptomeria planted on either side of the highway for a distance of 20 miles. These were set out by a poor man who was unable to contribute money toward the building of the temple. Today, this avenue of trees is more famous than the temple itself.

Cucumber-tree (*Magnolia acuminata*). Deciduous. Conical, with central leader. Moderately dense. Rate of growth, moderately rapid on moist ground. Zone 5.

Height. 60 to 80 feet.

Leaf, Flower, Fruit. Leaves are 5 to 10 inches long and about half as wide; dark green on upper surface, light green on lower. Flower petals are 2 to 3 inches long, greenish yellow. They appear in early June after the foliage has developed and frequently go unnoticed. Fruit is like a knobby cucumber, 3 inches long, turning from green to deep pink in September. Sections open to reveal bright red seeds on white elastic threads.

Culture. Deep, rich, moist soil. Fleshy roots, therefore difficult to transplant. Move with a ball of soil.

Habitat. Southern Alleghenies west to Arkansas.

Uses. Lawn specimen. Near a garden.

Comment. Shapely tree with large dark green leaves, a stately specimen. Flowers are the least showy of the magnolias but the seed pods are well displayed.

Devilwood (*Osmanthus americanus*). Broad-leaved evergreen shrub; older specimens may attain stature of a small tree. Irregularly rounded. Open. Rate of growth, rapid. Zone 7.

Height. 20 to 30 feet.

Leaf, Flower, Fruit. Leaves are 2 to 5 inches long, about one-third as wide; light green. Flowers open in early spring, are not showy but appear in large numbers and have pleasant lemon fragrance. Fruits are blue-black.

Culture. Deep soil with ample moisture. Semi-shade in the warmer parts of the South, sunny areas elsewhere. Few pests.

Habitat. North Carolina to Florida and Mississippi.

Uses. Open screen.

Comment. The fragrance of the flowers and the evergreen holly-like foliage are admired. Common name refers to the difficulty encountered in splitting the wood of this tree.

Dogwood, Flowering (*Cornus florida*). Deciduous. Older specimens are flat-topped and spreading. Rate of growth, moderate. Zone 5.

Height. 25 feet.

Leaf, Flower, Fruit.   Leaves are 3 to 4 inches long, 1½ to 3 inches wide; medium green, very light green on lower surface; scarlet in autumn except in moist soil where they may remain green until a hard frost withers them. The prominent white "flower," 3 to 4 inches across in mid-May, actually consists of four bracts. These are not as fragile as petals and persist for several weeks in spite of rainy or windy weather. Each bract is rounded and notched at the tip. Clusters of bright scarlet fruits appear in September and October.

Culture.   Well-drained site but with ample humus and summer moisture. Move with a ball of soil. Will grow in the shade but few flower buds will set unless there is ample light. It is slow to become fully established after transplanting, and flowering may be delayed for several years. Lawn specimens may be troubled by borers in trunk.

Habitat.   Eastern United States.

Uses.   Lawn specimen. Edge of woodland. Along streets, but supplemented by taller trees.

Comment.   It is widely planted and much admired. Outstanding in floral effect and good fall color of leaf and berries; noteworthy winter structure. State tree of Missouri, North Carolina, and Virginia.

Pink Flowering Dogwood (*Cornus florida rubra*) has deep pink bracts and the foliage is darker green than the type. Height, 25 feet. Zone 5*.

Welch Flowering Dogwood (*Cornus florida welchi*) has a light-colored, variegated leaf. Height, 25 feet. Zone 5.

Alternate-leaf Dogwood (*Cornus alternifolia*) does not have showy bracts; its fruit is small and blue-black; and unlike other dogwoods, its leaves are not arranged opposite each other along the twigs. Sometimes called Pagoda-tree. Height, 20 feet. Zone 4.

Dogwood, Japanese (*Cornus kousa*). Deciduous. Framework branches are ascending, smaller branches are horizontal. If some lower branches are left, the effect will be that of a multi-stemmed tree. Rate of growth, moderate. Zone 5*.

Height. 25 feet.

Leaf, Flower, Fruit, Bark.   Leaf is 3 inches long, no more than 1 inch wide; russet-red in late autumn. Unless it is on high ground, early frosts will cause leaves to turn brown. No petals, but the four long-pointed white bracts are showy and frequently last for several weeks in June. At first, bracts are small and green but develop larger size (1 to 2 inches long and ½ to ¾ inches wide) just at the time the bracts of the native flowering dogwood are dropping. The red fruit resembles a small strawberry. Flaking bark on mature specimens adds a color note that is of special interest during the winter.

Kwanzan Flowering Cherry, with its mass of bloom and delicacy of petal, is one of a Japanese tree group that people will travel many miles to see. (*Roche*)

Flowering Dogwood is widely admired for its floral display. Since the showy white or pink flowers are bracts, rather than petals, the color festival is prolonged. (*Grant Heilman*)

Culture. A well-drained loam. Leafmold or other form of humus near the root area is desirable.

Habitat. Japan and Korea.

Uses. Specimen. Attracts considerable attention since it flowers later than the more widely planted flowering dogwood.

Comment. Floral display, fruit, and bark have a three-season appeal. Sometimes called Kousa Dogwood and Pagoda Dogwood.

Chinese Dogwood (*Cornus kousa chinensis*) is similar except that the bracts are wider and somewhat overlapping. It is native to China. Height, 25 feet. Zone 5*.

Dogwood, Kousa, see **Dogwood, Japanese.**

Douglas-fir (*Pseudotsuga taxifolia*). Needle evergreen. Conical, comparatively narrow at the base, with a single leader. Moderately dense. Rate of growth, moderate. Zone 3*.

Height. 70 feet.

Leaf and Cone. Needles are ¾ to 1½ inches long, $\frac{1}{16}$ inch wide, flat, rounded at tip. Cones are 2½ to 4 inches long.

Culture. Quite tolerant if there is ample moisture. Withstands city conditions better than the hemlock. Transplants well but should be moved with a ball of soil.

Habitat. British Columbia to Texas, at high elevations.

Uses. Windbreak. Tall screen.

Comment. The blue-green type from Colorado may be more desirable than the dull green one from Vancouver. Douglas-fir does not have the high color effect of a blue spruce. May be used in Christmas tree plantations since it holds its needles well when used indoors. At one time it was known as *Pseudotsuga douglasi*. It is not a true fir although it looks like a small-needled version of one. The scientific name describes it as a false hemlock with yew-like foliage. Evidently the botanists had difficulty in classifying this plant, which has recently been renamed *Psuedotsuga menziesii*. The State tree of Oregon.

Elm, American (*Ulmus americana*). Deciduous. Shape is variable although it is usually highly arched. Rate of growth, moderately rapid. Zone 2.

Height. 90 feet.

Leaf. Leaves are 3 to 5 inches long and less than half as wide; dark green, turning yellow to russet in autumn.

Culture. Tolerant, but grows best in rich, moist soil. Fibrous root system, therefore easily transplanted.

Habitat. Canada to Florida and west to the Rockies.

Uses. Street tree for broad avenues. Lawn specimen.

Comment. The State tree of Massachusetts and Nebraska, the elm was once the most widely planted tree across the country, but serious diseases have curtailed its use. Dutch elm disease and phloem necrosis seem to be restricted primarily to elms. Phloem necrosis is the quicker acting and the more difficult to prevent. At present it is found only in the Midwest, whereas Dutch elm disease is found over a wide area. Once a tree has become infected with either disease there is as of now no cure. However, considerable research is in progress for control of these troubles. Unfortunately, there are some so-called tree experts who are not averse to claiming to have a control for these diseases, and they sell their services and products at an exorbitant rate to a public that understandably is anxious to save its choice elms.

There are some preventive steps that can be taken. One is sanitation; that is, the removing and burning of diseased and weakened trees. (The wood which is removed should not be stored for home use since the beetles live underneath the old bark and emerge to attack another tree.) Another is spraying, to control the elm bark beetles that carry the diseases from one tree to another. One spray should be applied in early spring before the leaves emerge and another in early summer. This work should be done on a community-wide basis.

Tree experts are searching for a strain of American elm that is immune, or at least resistant, to these diseases, and there is some reason to think that such a tree will be found.

Christine Buisman Elm is a selection of the Smooth-leaved Elm (*Ulmus carpinifolia*) that is noted for its resistance to diseases that attack other elms. It does not have the vase shape of the American elm, however. In some areas it is slow to establish itself as an attractive specimen. Height, 70 feet. Zone 5.

Elm, Camperdown (*Ulmus glabra camperdowni*). Deciduous. Broad-spreading, irregularly flat-topped. Outer branches are pendulous. Rate of growth, moderate. Zone 5.

Height. 20 feet.

Leaf. Leaves are 3 to 6 inches long and about half as wide; dark green, and of rough texture.

Culture. Tolerant of a variety of soils. Full sun. Easily transplanted. Subject to Dutch elm disease and the leaf-eating insects that attack the American elm.

Habitat. Garden form was found in Scotland.

Uses. For a collector's garden, or for a place where a small pendulous tree of bold form is desirable.

Comment. This is a stiffly pendulous tree that is grafted onto a straight-trunked elm some 6 to 8 feet from the ground. It is a horticultural variety of Scotch Elm (*Ulmus glabra*).

Elm, Chinese (*Ulmus parvifolia*). Deciduous; semi-evergreen in the South. Round-topped. Dense. Rate of growth, moderately fast. Zone 6.
Height. 40 to 50 feet.
Leaf, Flower, Bark. Leaves are ¾ to 2 inches long and half as wide, with sawtoothed edge; dark green, and held late without change of color. Small flowers appear in late summer. Bark is mottled; flakes off, showing areas of light-colored inner bark.
Culture. Tolerant. Easily transplanted. Few pests.
Habitat. China and Japan.
Uses. Lawn tree.
Comment. Superior to Siberian elm, which has been widely sold as "Chinese" elm.

Elm, Gray-barked, see **Zelkova.**

Elm, Siberian (*Ulmus pumila*). Deciduous. Irregularly round-headed. Quite open. Rate of growth, very rapid. Zone 3*.
Height. 70 feet.
Leaf, Flower, Bark. Leaves are ¾ to 3 inches long and half as wide, with double or triple sawtoothed edge; dark green, dropping without much change of color in autumn. Small flowers open in late March. Fine twigs. Bark is light colored.
Culture. Tolerant. Dry site. Transplants readily. Branches are easily broken in storms. Few pests.
Habitat. Eastern Siberia, northern China.
Uses. A temporary lawn tree that should be removed after a few years.
Comment. Widely planted because of its rapid growth. It is better suited to the dry Plains States than to other areas. Incorrectly, although generally, called Chinese Elm, which is the common name of *Ulmus parvifolia*.

Enkianthus, Redvein (*Enkianthus campanulatus*). Deciduous shrub; older specimens may attain stature of a small tree. Upright in form. Rate of growth, moderate. Zone 5.
Height. 15 to 20 feet.
Leaf, Flower, Bark. Leaf is bright green with red petiole, 2 inches long, 1½ inches wide; yellow to orange-red in late autumn. Flowers

are bell-shaped, cream with red veining, mid-May. Old wood is smooth and a light yellow-gray.

Culture.   Acid soil with ample moisture.

Habitat.   Japan.

Uses.   Screen. Near buildings where an upright plant is needed.

Comment.   This relative of the azalea has a clean, attractive appearance at all times. Fall coloring is outstanding.

Fir, White (*Abies concolor*). Needle evergreen. Conical, branched to the base. Quite dense. Rate of growth, fairly rapid. Zone 4.

Height.   75 feet.

Leaf and Cone.   Needles are 1 to 2 inches long, $\frac{1}{10}$ of an inch wide, flat; light gray-green on both sides. Erect cones to 4 inches long may be purplish when young.

Culture.   Loam. Well-drained site but plant does require moisture. Has fibrous roots. Move with a ball of soil. Few pests.

Habitat.   Colorado to New Mexico.

Uses.   Lawn specimen.

Comment.   Resembles blue spruce but is a softer color, less severe in outline, and less subject to insect and disease attack. Lends itself to cultivation in eastern United States better than other firs, which cannot withstand dry summers. See also Douglas-fir.

Franklinia (*Franklinia alatamaha*). Deciduous. Irregular outline. Upright, with several stems, becoming wider at the top. Quite open. Rate of growth, moderately slow. Zone 6*.

Height.   20 to 30 feet.

Leaf and Flower.   Leaves are 5 to 6 inches long, less than half as wide; shiny dark green above and light green below, turning a bright orange-red in autumn. Flowers are white, 2 to 3 inches across, on short stalks, appearing in September and October, a few opening each day.

Culture.   Rich soil, with humus. Needs summer moisture.

Habitat.   Georgia.

Uses.   For collectors because of its historic interest, or as part of a garden in warmer sections.

Comment.   John Bartram, the famed naturalist, found this tree in 1770 and sent it to his botanical garden in Philadelphia. It has not been found as a native since 1790. It was named in honor of Benjamin Franklin. It is late flowering, and even when buds set on plants grown in its northern limits they may fail to open. Sometimes called Lost Plant. Formerly known as Gordonia.

Fringe-tree (*Chionanthus virginica*). Deciduous shrub; older specimens may attain stature of a small tree. Irregular, taller than broad. Rate of growth, slow. Zone 5.

Height.   20 feet.

Leaf, Flower, Fruit.   Leaves are 2 to 8 inches long and less than half as wide; medium dark green. Flowers are white in loose clusters up to 8 inches long, each petal being 1 inch long and no more than ¼ inch wide; early June. Fruit is dark blue, ½ to ¾ inch long. Male form has the better flower display but produces no fruit.

Culture.   Tolerant, but moist sandy soil is preferred. Scale may be troublesome.

Habitat.   Pennsylvania to Texas.

Uses.   For large lawn areas.

Comment.   Distinctive flowers are produced in profusion at a time when few woody plants are in bloom. The tree is of rather coarse texture and is very late to leaf out in the spring so that to the unknowing it appears to be dead. Formerly known as *Chionanthus virginicus*.

Ginkgo (*Ginkgo biloba*). Deciduous. Mature tree is broad, round-headed, quite regular in outline; younger tree is quite irregular. Rate of growth, slow. Zone 4*.

Height.   80 feet.

Leaf, Flower, Fruit, Bark.   Leaves are fan-shaped and often 2-lobed, 3 inches wide and 2 to 3 inches long; light green. In the autumn they turn a clear bright yellow and all seem to fall at about the same time. Male and female flowers are on separate plants; young trees produce no flowers. Fruit is 1 to 1½ inches long, yellowish green, and plum-shaped, with unpleasant odor. Trunk is light colored.

Culture.   Very tolerant; does well in cities. Fibrous root system, therefore easily moved even in larger sizes. Few, if any, pests; even wood-rotting diseases are rare.

Habitat.   Eastern China.

Uses.   Lawn specimen. Street tree.

Comment.   A "living fossil," this species of tree existed 125 million years ago. It is the only living member of a once dominant race of vegetation. It belongs to the age of the dinosaur. There are specimens in Japan that are thought to be almost a thousand years of age. Because the foul-smelling fruit is undesirable, male clones are recommended. These non-fruiting selections are offered by a few nurserymen. Sometimes called Maidenhair-tree since the shape of the leaf resembles that of a maidenhair fern.

Goldenchain, Waterer (*Laburnum watereri*). Deciduous. Broad, columnar. Quite open. Rate of growth, moderate. Zone 5*.

Height. 25 feet.

Leaf, Flower, Bark. Trifoliate leaf, each leaflet 1½ inches long and less than 1 inch wide. Petioles are long, up to 2 inches. Flowers are bright yellow in long clusters much like wisteria; late May. Twigs and even older branches are greenish brown, giving winter interest.

Culture. Ample moisture. Soil not too acid, well drained. Light shade desired; full sun may burn foliage. Trunk may split if exposed to excess cold. Few pests.

Habitat. Hybrid origin. Parent plants were native to Europe.

Uses. Near a house since it is not wide spreading. Background for a garden.

Comment. A plant with interest at all times; attractive flowers for spring, neat foliage pattern for summer, and for winter, twig color and clean lines as a result of sparse branching. Sometimes known as *Laburnum vossi*.

Goldenrain-tree (*Koelreuteria paniculata*). Deciduous. Rounded, slightly irregular. Not dense. Rate of growth, slow. Zone 6.

Height. 30 feet.

Leaf, Flower, Fruit. Leaves are compound, up to 15 inches long, with each leaflet 1 to 3 inches long and coarsely toothed or lobed; deep bright green. Small yellow flowers are in large upright clusters in mid-July. Fruit is inflated pod, 2 inches long, changing from pale green to pinkish cream to brown.

Culture. Tolerant, except to poorly drained conditions; withstands heat and drought. Readily transplanted. Does well in the city.

Habitat. China, Korea, Japan.

Uses. Lawn specimen. Street tree.

Comment. The flowers arrive when little else is in bloom, but they drop quickly. The seed pods are attractive and long lasting. Sometimes called Japanese Varnish-tree and Pride-of-India.

Gordonia, see Franklinia.

Gum, Black or **Sour, see Pepperidge.**

Hardy-orange (*Poncirus trifoliata*). Deciduous. Irregular outline unless pruned. Rate of growth, moderate. Zone 6*.

Height. 20 to 30 feet.

Leaf, Flower, Fruit, Bark. Dark green, leathery leaf is trifoliate, the largest leaflet 1½ inches long. Flowers are 2 inches in diameter,

The American Elm with its high arching branches gracefully enframes a house, a wide street, or a view. (*George Taloumis*)

Small areas need trees that will not grow too large. Goldenrain-tree is a good example of a shade tree of medium height. (*Paul E. Genereux*)

white, fragrant, appearing in late April. Two-inch golden fruit looks like a small orange. Twigs are green, with green, broadly triangular thorns up to 2 inches long.

Culture. Tolerant of varying light and soil conditions, even thriving on infertile soil. Responds well to restrictive pruning.

Habitat. Central and northern China.

Uses. Screen. Trimmed hedge.

Comment. Fruit offers colorful display. The thorns are decorative but can be a nuisance if plant is near a pathway.

Hawthorn, Cockspur (*Crataegus crus-galli*). Deciduous. Older specimens develop a flat top, and with the wide-spreading branches appearing in stratified layers, an attractive horizontal effect is presented. Rate of growth, moderate. Zone 5.

Height. 25 feet.

Leaf, Flower, Fruit. Dark green leaves, 3 inches long and 1¾ inches wide, are glossy; orange-red in autumn. White flowers in late May have an unpleasant odor. Bright red fruit, almost ½ inch in diameter, is produced in quantity and persists well into the winter. Numerous thorns are long and slender.

Culture. The hawthorns are tolerant but do better on a heavy soil than on one that is sandy; and the best ones are to be seen where the soil is not acid. Because of the taproot, it is advisable to start with small plants.

Habitat. Quebec to North Carolina and Kansas.

Uses. Can be used as a hedge or as an informal border plant where a thorny plant is desired. To give definition to an area several plants may be grouped together, the tops pruned to a uniform height (4 to 6 feet) and the lower branches pruned away to reveal the trunk and lower stems.

Comment. The dark glossy foliage is noteworthy. Fall color of foliage and berries is good. The State flower of Missouri.

Lavalle Hawthorn (*Crataegus lavallei*) is noted for its red-orange berries which are held throughout the winter. Height, 25 feet. Zone 5.

Hawthorn, Paul's Scarlet (*Crataegus oxyacantha pauli*). Deciduous. Round-topped; numerous small twigs. Dense. Rate of growth, moderate. Zone 5.

Height. 20 feet.

Leaf and Flower. Leaf is shallowly lobed, ½ to 2 inches long and about the same width; dark green and held late without change of color. Flower is bright pink, somewhat over ½ inch in diameter; late May. Scattered thorns are 1 inch long.

Culture. Heavy, dry loam. Slow to become established. Plant with ball of soil. Leaf-blight is troublesome on lighter soils and in the more humid atmospere of eastern portions of the country.
Habitat. Originated in England.
Uses. Lawn specimen. Street tree. Garden tree.
Comment. Where this grows well it is a favorite.
Columnar Hawthorn (*Crataegus monogyna stricta*) is noted for its dense columnar form, the branches being erect. Height, 20 feet. Zone 5.

Hawthorn, Washington (*Crataegus phaenopyrum*). Deciduous. Round-headed; compact. Rate of growth, moderate. Zone 5.
Height. 30 feet.
Leaf, Flower, Fruit. Leaf is 2 to 4 inches long, ¾ to 1¾ inches wide, 3- to 5-lobed; shiny, deep green with reddish cast at the tip; medium-fine texture; brilliant scarlet in the fall. Spines are 2½ inches long. Flowers, in late May, and fruit resemble those of cockspur hawthorn.
Culture. See notations under Cockspur Hawthorn. Withstands city conditions. Grows well where winters are cold and dry; not at its best in coastal areas.
Habitat. Virginia to Alabama and Missouri.
Uses. See Cockspur Hawthorn.
Comment. Naturally dense. One of the better hawthorns because of its rather small and glossy leaf.

Hemlock, Canada (*Tsuga canadensis*). Needle evergreen. Graceful habit with its spiry top and slender drooping twigs. Rate of growth, moderately rapid. Zone 3.
Height. 75 feet.
Leaf and Cone. Needles, which are ⅜ inch long, are dark green and this coloring appears to intensify during the winter. Twigs are willowy so that ice or sleet storms seldom break them. Cones are less than an inch long.
Culture. Deep, moist loam, well drained. Withstands considerable shade. Does poorly on a site exposed to strong winds. Spring moving is recommended. Red spider may infest the south side of plants in a dry location.
Habitat. Southern Canada, the Northeast, the Lake States, and the Appalachian Mountains.
Uses. Informal screen. Sheared hedge.
Comment. Because of its fine foliage and twigs it lends itself very well to pruning. If upper branches are cut back while they are less than 1 inch in diameter and if the side branches are nipped back, the size

can be restrained to 25 feet, yet the natural gracefulness of the tree will be retained.

Numerous horticultural selections have been found. These range in habit from dense types to slow-growing dwarfs to arching shrub forms, and even to a spreading ground-cover variety. With the exception of the Sargent Weeping Hemlock, they are available for the most part only as small specimens for the plant collector. The State tree of Pennsylvania.

Sargent Weeping Hemlock (*Tsuga canadensis pendula*) is broad spreading and pendulous, giving a fountain-like effect. Height, 15 feet. Zone 3.

Hemlock, Carolina (*Tsuga caroliniana*). Needle evergreen. Graceful habit; slender drooping twigs. Rate of growth, moderate. Zone 5.

Height. 50 feet.

Leaf and Cone. The needles, ½ inch long, are a darker green and grow more uniformly around the twig than do those of the Canada hemlock. Carolina is a more compact plant than the Canada hemlock. Cones are an inch or more long.

Culture. See notations under Canada Hemlock. Carolina hemlock is reputed to withstand city conditions better. It takes longer to become established than the other does.

Habitat. Mountains of southwestern Virginia to Georgia.

Uses. As a specimen tree or as a hedge.

Comment. The dark green foliage and the lacy outline of the tree give it distinction.

Hemlock, Japanese (*Tsuga diversifolia*). Needle evergreen. Broadly oval with irregular top. Dense. Rate of growth, slow. Zone 6.

Height. 35 feet.

Leaf and Cone. Needles are ½ inch long, $\frac{1}{16}$ inch wide, dark green. Young needles in a tight rosette contrast with older foliage. Cones are ½ to ¾ inch long.

Culture. Deep, moist loam, well drained. Spring moving is recommended.

Habitat. Japan.

Uses. Lawn specimen. Screen.

Comment. Compared to the Canada hemlock, it is a darker green, is more dense, and does not grow as tall. Not commonly seen.

Holly, American (*Ilex opaca*). Broad-leaved evergreen. Conical; retains its lower branches. Dense. Older specimens become more open. Rate of growth, slow. Zone 6.

Height. 40 to 50 feet. (Of lesser size in its northern limits.)

Leaf and Fruit. Leaves are 3 inches long and 1¾ inches wide;

spine-toothed; deep dull green compared to the glossy leaf of the tender English holly. Red berries persist throughout the winter. Fruiting is dependent upon having both male and female plants.

Culture. Well-drained, rich, sandy soil with additional humus worked in at time of planting. Do not allow the soil to become excessively dry. Older plants are difficult to transplant unless extra precautions are taken. Leaf miner may attack.

Habitat. Massachusetts to Florida, west to Missouri and Texas. It is at its best on Cape Cod and in New Jersey and Virginia.

Uses. Gives touch of high quality near corners of a large house or some 15 feet away from a smaller residence.

Comment. The red berries and the distinctive leaves are widely admired. Numerous clones are now being tried, some selected for greater hardiness, others for better fruiting, more attractive foliage, and better plant shape, which varies from tree form to narrowly upright to shrubby. The State tree of Delaware.

Holly, Dahoon (*Ilex cassine*). Broad-leaved evergreen shrub; older specimens may attain stature of a small tree. Irregularly upright. Generally a single trunk. Dense when grown in the sun. Rate of growth, moderately rapid. Zone 7*.

Height. 15 to 20 feet.

Leaf, Fruit, Bark. Leaves are 1½ to 4 inches long and no more than one-third as wide, with smooth edge; dark green. Male and female flowers are on separate plants. Fruits are red, ¼ inch in diameter, in clusters. Bark is gray.

Culture. Either wet or normal soils. Withstands some shade. Few pests.

Habitat. Virginia to Florida and Louisiana.

Uses. Screen.

Comment. Abundance of red berries. Will grow on poorly drained soils.

Foster Holly (*Ilex fosteri*), a hybrid between dahoon and American holly, has a leaf similar to the American except that it is glossy. It is noted for rapid growth and heavy fruit production. Height, 15 to 20 feet. Zone 6.

Holly, Japanese (*Ilex crenata*). Broad-leaved evergreen shrub; older specimens may attain stature of a small tree. Habit of growth is upright. Moderately dense. Rate of growth, slow. Zone 6*.

Height. 20 feet.

Leaf and Fruit. Leaves are elliptical in shape with no spines; 1 inch long and ½ inch wide; very dark green and somewhat glossy. Fruit is small, black, inconspicuous. The plant resembles a boxwood more than a traditional holly.

Culture. Tolerant of a variety of soil and light conditions. Severe winters will damage young plants in particular. Plants near a windy corner of a building or in an open field are also subject to injury. Pests are rarely troublesome.

Habitat. Japan.

Uses. To gain height without undue massiveness. Use at corners of building or garden.

Comment. The small leaves give a distinctive appearance. Because of its small twigs it lends itself to shearing for compactness.

Holly, Yaupon (*Ilex vomitoria*). Broad-leaved evergreen shrub; older specimens may attain stature of a small tree. Upright, conical, generally multi-stemmed. Fairly dense. Rate of growth, moderately rapid. Zone 7*.

Height. 15 to 20 feet.

Leaf, Fruit, Bark. Leaves are ½ to 1½ inches long and about half as wide, with slightly toothed margin; dark green, glossy. Male and female flowers are on separate plants. Fruit is scarlet, less than ¼ inch in diameter. Bark is gray.

Culture. Tolerant. Will withstand wet soils. Good near seashore. Few pests.

Habitat. Virginia to Florida, west to Texas.

Uses. Screen.

Comment. An evergreen plant of medium-fine texture producing an abundance of red berries.

Honey-locust, Thornless (*Gleditsia triacanthos inermis*). Deciduous. Broad, round-headed. Very open. Rate of growth, moderately rapid. Zone 4*.

Height. 70 to 80 feet.

Leaf, Flower. Fruit. Leaves are doubly compound, up to 8 inches long, with 15 to 30 leaflets; each leaflet is usually 1½ inches long and less than ½ inch wide; bright emerald green, turning to clear yellow in autumn. Flowers are not showy. Seed pods are dark, shiny brown, and may be over a foot long and 1½ inches wide.

Culture. Very tolerant; withstands drought. Readily transplanted. At one time it was thought to be free of pests, but lately locust mite has caused premature foliage drop.

Habitat. Central United States.

Uses. Shade tree for large lawn areas.

Comment. Common Honey-locust (*Gleditsia triacanthos*) has strong thorns as long as 4 inches, usually branched, and frequently appearing on the trunk as well as on young wood. In recent years, however, thornless and non-fruiting clones have become available. Moraine ® Honey-locust (Plant Patent 836) was the first of these, but frequently it takes several years to develop a good root system and it tends to be more spreading than upright. More recent selections of thornless honey-locust that have overcome these disadvantages are Shademaster (Plant Patent 1515), Imperial (Plant Patent 1605), and Skyline (Plant Patent 1619). Shademaster withstands seashore and city conditions and may be used as a street tree. All of the honey-locusts are noted for their fine texture. They provide a light shade. Leaf canopy and root system are compatible with a good lawn. Autumn raking is not necessary since the leaflets curl up as they fall.

Sunburst Honey-locust (*Gleditsia triacanthos inermis* 'Sunburst') (Plant Patent 1313) has bright yellow foliage at the ends of the twigs. Height about 60 feet. Zone 4*.

Hornbeam, European (*Carpinus betulus*). Deciduous. Globular. Compact with many small twigs. Retains lower branches. Rate of growth, slow. Zone 5.
Height. 50 feet.
Leaf and Bark. Leaves are 1½ to 3½ inches long, 1 to 2 inches wide; dark green. They turn a light yellow in autumn, later change to brown, and may persist into early winter. Smooth dark gray bark resembles that of the beech.
Culture. Will grow in the poorer soils if they are not too acid and are well drained. Fibrous roots. Moves well as a small plant but not easily as a larger specimen.
Habitat. Europe and Iran.
Uses. Near a large building where a lightly sheared plant is desired. In a large formal garden.
Comment. When lightly sheared, its neat, compact form is accentuated.
Pyramid European Hornbeam (*Carpinus betulus fastigiata*) is a good small columnar tree. Height, 30 feet. Zone 5.

Hornbeam, Hop (*Ostrya virginiana*). Deciduous. Broadly rounded. Moderately open. Rate of growth, very slow. Zone 5.
Height. 30 feet.
Leaf, Fruit, Bark. Leaves are 2 to 4½ inches long, 1 to 2 inches wide; medium green, changing to a brownish yellow in autumn. Seeds appear in clusters similar to those of the hop, and are 1½ to 2½ inches long. Slender twigs. Bark is light grayish brown with narrow pieces that curl up at the lower end.

Culture. Tolerant. Withstands dry conditions very well. Fibrous roots; transplants well as a young plant or as a nursery-grown specimen. Few pests.

Habitat. Eastern North America.

Uses. Near edge of woods or under high-branched trees. Street tree for narrow planting areas.

Comment. Moderately fine texture and a small trunk sets this tree apart. It is one of several trees that are sometimes called Ironwood.

Ironwood, see **Hop Hornbeam.**

Japanese Keaki, see **Zelkova.**

Japanese Pagoda-tree, see **Chinese Scholar-tree.**

Japanese Varnish-tree, see **Goldenrain-tree.**

Judas-tree, see **Redbud, Eastern.**

Juniper, Blue Columnar Chinese (*Juniperus chinensis columnaris*). Needle evergreen. Broad, columnar. Dense. Rate of growth, moderate. Zone 4.

Height. 25 feet.

Leaf and Fruit. Needles are ¼ inch long, sharp pointed; silvery green. Fruits are ¼ inch in diameter, light blue-green.

Culture. Well-drained soil, full sun. Move with ball of soil in spring. Pests include bagworm and red spider.

Habitat. China and Japan.

Uses. Accent. Screen.

Comment. Best of the silvery green columnar evergreens.

Keteleer juniper (*Juniperus chinensis keteleeri*), a horticultural selection sometimes listed as a variety of red-cedar, retains a good green throughout the year. Its fruit is large and light blue. Height, 25 feet. Zone 4.

Katsura (*Cercidiphyllum japonicum*). Deciduous. Female tree, broadly ovate; male, broadly columnar. Dense. Rate of growth, moderately rapid in early years. Zone 4*.

Height. 40 feet.

Leaf and Flower. Rounded leaves are 2 to 3 inches in diameter; deep bluish green above, lighter underneath; reddish in spring and usually yellow, but may be reddish, in autumn. Male and female flowers are on separate plants. Neither they nor the fruits are showy.

Culture. Rich, moist but well-drained soil. Moves readily with ball of soil. If soil is dry, leaves drop in late summer. Seldom troubled by pests.

Habitat. Japan.

Uses. Columnar form for screen or accent. Ovate form for lawn specimen.

Comment. A neat tree of moderate size and medium-fine texture that could well be more widely used.

Lilac (*Syringa vulgaris*). Deciduous shrub; older specimens may attain stature of a small tree. Upright, irregular in outline. Rate of growth, moderately rapid. Zone 3*.

Height. 20 feet.

Leaf and Flower. Leaf is bluish green, to 4 inches long and 3 inches wide. Flowers are lilac or white in large upright clusters, fragrant; mid-May. Hybrids offer wider range of color.

Culture. Tolerant of a variety of conditions but is at its best in limestone soils; does not like "wet feet." Easily transplanted. Scale, borers, and powdery mildew may be troublesome. The mildew detracts from the appearance of the plant, otherwise does little harm. Plants growing in full sun with a good circulation of air are less subject to mildew. Hybrids that are established on their own roots are better than grafted plants.

Habitat. Southeastern Europe.

Uses. Screen.

Comment. Showy flowers have a great appeal. It is not noteworthy at other seasons but its popularity continues year after year. State flower of New Hampshire.

The well-known French "hybrids" are not hybrids in the true sense; rather, they are horticultural selections, and although some originated in France, many more are of American origin. These selections have a wide range of color, and there are double-flowered ones as well as singles. In some instances, they are not fragrant. More than 500 named forms have been listed. A few that are outstanding are Ludwig Spaeth (single purple), Congo (single magenta), Mrs. Edward Harding (double magenta), Belle de Nancy (double pink), President Lincoln (single bluish purple), Mont Blanc (single white), Ellen Willmott (double white).

Lilac, Japanese Tree (*Syringa amurensis japonica*). Deciduous. Broad, oval, dense. Rate of growth, moderate. Zone 5.

Height. 30 feet.

Leaf, Flower, Bark. Leaves are 3 to 6 inches long and about half as wide; dark green. Flowers are creamy white in loose clusters 12

Japanese Hemlock is a graceful, compact tree with dark green foliage. (*Paul E. Genereux*)

Japanese Tree Lilac is, in truth, a tree. In June it is covered with large clusters of creamy white flowers. (*Paul E. Genereux*)

inches long, with unpleasant aroma at close range; mid-June. Bark is smooth reddish brown and has light-colored horizontal lines.

Culture. Tolerant. Withstands cold temperatures and dry weather.

Habitat. Japan.

Uses. Lawn or garden specimen. Street tree.

Comment. The foliage and trunk coloring are more interesting than those of the common lilac. It is a small tree of good shape.

Lily-of-the-valley-tree, see **Sorrel-tree.**

Linden, Little-leaf (*Tilia cordata*). Deciduous. Oval, dense. Rate of growth, moderately slow. Zone 4*.

Height. 60 feet.

Leaf and Flower. Leaves are rounded, indented at base, 1½ to 3 inches wide. Small yellowish white flowers are fragrant in early July; much sought after by bees.

Culture. Tolerant of a variety of soils; requires fair amount of moisture. Does well in the city. Fibrous root system, therefore easily moved. It is one of the favorite foods of Japanese beetles.

Habitat. Europe.

Uses. Lawn specimen. Street tree. Since it retains a compact habit without pruning and has dark green foliage, it can be used for planting formal approaches to a building. May be clipped for a greater degree of formality.

Comment. A stately, neat tree, with a small leaf.

Crimean Linden (*Tilia euchlora*) is another small-leaved species from Europe, with a glossier leaf. The European lindens are the lime-trees of English literature. Height, 60 feet. Zone 4*.

Linden, Silver (*Tilia tomentosa*). Deciduous. Broad, oval, dense. Rate of growth, moderately rapid. Zone 4.

Height. 60 to 80 feet.

Leaf and Flower. Leaves are 3 to 5 inches long and about as wide; deep green with some gloss; lower surface whitish and fuzzy. No change of color in autumn. Small yellowish white flowers are fragrant in early July.

Culture. Tolerant. Withstands heat and drought. Easily transplanted.

Habitat. Southeastern Europe to western Asia.

Uses. Lawn specimen. Street tree.

Comment. A stately tree enlivened by the light-colored undersurface of the leaves. Sometimes called Silver Lime.

Magnolia, Hokkaido (*Magnolia kobus borealis*). Deciduous. Broad, round head. Dense. Rate of growth, moderately rapid. Zone 5.

Height. 50 feet.

Leaf, Flower, Fruit. Leaves are 2½ to 4 inches long, less than half as wide, tapered at the base; dark green above, light green on lower side. Flowers are white, 5 inches in diameter, 6 to 9 petals; late April. Typical magnolia fruit (see Saucer Magnolia).

Culture. Tolerant, but requires good drainage. Must be moved with ball of soil. Few pests, although the soft magnolia scale may be troublesome.

Habitat. Japan.

Uses. Lawn specimen. Street tree.

Comment. Largest of the showy-flowered deciduous magnolias. Hardier than *Magnolia kobus*. Does not flower as a young plant.

Magnolia, Saucer (*Magnolia soulangeana*). Deciduous. Broad, rounded, retains lower branches. Dense. Rate of growth, moderate. Zone 5*.

Height. 25 feet.

Leaf, Flower, Fruit, Bark. Leaves are dark green, 5 to 7 inches long, 3 to 4 inches wide, leathery. They turn a pleasing brown in late autumn and do not wither before dropping. Cup-shaped flowers are white with underside of outer petals pink or reddish purple, 6 inches across; early May. Fruit resembles an irregular cucumber, green turning red, opening to show bright red seeds. Flower buds are gray and fuzzy, resembling large pussywillow catkins, and are on display throughout the winter. The trunk and stems are smooth and light gray-brown, providing winter interest also.

Culture. Rich soil, slightly acid, well drained. Sun. Do not plant in low areas which are subject to late frosts because once the flower buds start to open they are easily damaged. Withstands city conditions. Fleshy root, therefore must be moved with a ball of soil. Pests are rare.

Habitat. Hybrid, originating in France.

Uses. Specimen for lawn or large garden.

Comment. On a four-season basis, few plants can compare with its consistently high rating. Too sophisticated in appearance for rural settings. Some selections have a deeper pink coloring.

Lennei Magnolia (*Magnolia soulangeana lennei*) has a thick petal of dark reddish purple in a sculptured effect. Lennei flowers later than the type. Height, 25 feet. Zone 5*.

Magnolia, Southern (*Magnolia grandiflora*). Broad-leaved evergreen. Conical; lower branches are retained if there is sufficient light. Rate of growth, moderately slow. Zone 7*.

Height.   80 to 90 feet.

Leaf and Flower.   Leaves are glossy and very dark green, leathery, 5 to 8 inches long and less than half as wide. Flowers of 8-inch diameter are white and fragrant, late May, with scattered flowers throughout the summer.

Culture.   Good garden soil; ample moisture preferred. Flourishes where summer temperatures are high. When tried in the northern limit of its hardiness it will not grow as tall, and it should be used near a large building for protection from drying winds.

Habitat.   North Carolina to Florida and Texas, especially coastal lowlands.

Uses.   Lawn specimen. Street tree. Effective espaliered against a large brick surface.

Comment.   A tree in which the South takes great pride. The handsome foliage and the large outstanding flower give it prominence among other plantings. Sometimes called Bull Bay or Great Laurel. The State tree of Louisiana and Mississippi.

Magnolia, Star (*Magnolia stellata*). Deciduous. Round-topped, dense. Rate of growth, moderately slow. Zone 5*.

Height.   20 feet.

Leaf, Flower, Fruit, Bark.   Leaf is medium green, up to 2½ inches long and less than 1 inch wide; smallest of the magnolias. Flowers are white, with 15 or more narrow strap-like petals; fragrant; late April. Flower bud and fruit are similar to saucer magnolia but smaller. Twigs are of light color and of smaller dimension than saucer magnolia.

Culture.   Same as saucer magnolia. Few pests, but a soft scale is sometimes found.

Habitat.   Japan.

Uses.   Garden. Espalier. Near small house if restrictive pruning is practiced. Can be kept to half its normal height yet will retain its natural appearance if small upright branches are cut back annually.

Comment.   Leaf is smaller than that of other magnolias and the plant is therefore easier to blend with other plantings. Flower buds are winter hardy but they open early in the season and once the protective scales are broken the petals are sensitive to late frosts.

Pink Star Magnolia (*Magnolia stellata rosea*) has deep pink flowers. Height, 20 feet. Zone 5*.

Waterlily Magnolia (*M. s.* 'Waterlily') has twice as many petals, not as long as the type, and it flowers ten days later. Height, 20 feet. Zone 5*.

Magnolia, Sweet-bay (*Magnolia virginiana*). Semi-evergreen in the North, evergreen in the South. Irregular, generally multi-stemmed, quite open. Rate of growth, moderately slow. Zone 5*.

Height.   20 feet.

Leaf, Flower, Fruit, Bark.   Leaves are elliptical, 3 to 6 inches long and 1½ to 2 inches wide; glossy dark green, very white beneath. It is late to leaf out in the spring but holds its leaves, especially in a protected place, very late in the autumn. No change of color. White flowers, 2 to 3 inches across, turn deep cream color; fragrant. The tree blooms in late May with scattered flowers throughout the summer. Fruit resembles a knobby cucumber, opens to show bright red seeds on elastic strings. Twigs are bright green.

Culture.   Rich, moist soil. Will grow on poorly drained site. Fleshy roots, therefore move with ball of soil. Few pests.

Habitat.   Coastal area of eastern United States as far north as Massachusetts.

Uses.   As underplanting at edge of woods; or where a small, open, irregular tree is needed. Provides good silhouette. Combines well with dwarf yews. Looks well against a red brick surface.

Comment.   The rich foliage and relatively small, cup-shaped flowers are classical in appearance. Formerly known as *Magnolia glauca*.

Maidenhair-tree, see **Ginkgo.**

Maple, Bloodleaf Japanese (*Acer palmatum atropurpureum*). Deciduous. Round-headed but with irregular branching. Multi-stemmed, or at least gives this effect if low side branches are retained and branchlets are removed near base of tree. Rate of growth, moderate. Zone 6.

Height.   20 feet.

Leaf and Fruit.   Leaves are 2 to 3½ inches long and of similar width; distinctive, with 5 to 7 sharply pointed lobes; red, assuming brightest tones when they unfold in the spring and again in the autumn. The red keys or seed pods are attractive.

Culture.   Well-drained, good garden soil. Sun most of day is required for best leaf color. Move with a ball of soil, preferably in the spring.

Habitat.   Korea and Japan.

Uses.   Lawn specimen.

Comment.   The leaf outline is striking and makes an interesting shadow pattern against a wall or paving.

Bloodgood is noted as a variety that retains a deeper color throughout the summer than most others.

Japanese Maple (*Acer palmatum*), the original species, has normally green leaves. It is rarely seen, which is unfortunate since it harmonizes with a greater variety of settings. It makes an effective backdrop for a garden. Height, 20 feet. Zone 6.

Maple, Hedge (*Acer campestre*). Deciduous. Compact and globe-shaped, stately, small. Dense. Rate of growth, slow. Zone 5.
Height. 25 feet.
Leaf. Small rounded leaf, shallowly 3- to 5-lobed with rounded tips; moderately thick; dark green. Little fall color but may turn a yellow or yellow-brown late in the season. Numerous small twigs.
Culture. Good, well-drained soil. Will withstand city conditions. Sun or light shade. Good fibrous root system; transplants well. Should not be pruned in early spring or it will bleed; that is, excess sap will exude from cut twigs. Pests are rarely troublesome.
Habitat. Europe, western Asia.
Uses. Small stately tree for garden areas. Street tree.
Comment. No pruning required to maintain it as a compact tree. Sometimes known as English Maple.

Maple, Norway (*Acer platanoides*). Deciduous. Broad, oval, regular in outline. Dense. Rate of growth, moderately rapid. Zone 4.
Height. 50 to 70 feet.
Leaf and Flower. Leaves are dark green, 4 inches long and 5 inches wide, 5-lobed. They hold their green color until late in the season, then turn yellowish before dropping. Flowers are yellow-green in late April, appearing in large clusters just before the leaves come out; the most showy of the maple flowers.
Culture. Tolerates poor soil and will withstand city conditions better than other maples. Easily transplanted. Aphids may infest, causing honey-dew drip on the street.
Habitat. Europe and western Asia.
Uses. Primarily a street tree, but see comment below.
Comment. With its heavy shade and numerous surface roots, the regular Norway maple is incompatible with good lawns and other small plantings. Horticultural selections of *Acer platanoides* may be used for these purposes, however, and five are listed here.
Cleveland Maple is of oval-upright form with a spread of 20 to 25 feet. May be used as a lawn specimen or as a street tree. Height, 50 to 70 feet. Zone 4.
Crimson King Maple (Plant Patent 735) with its red summer foliage can be used as a lawn specimen. Height, 50 feet. Zone 4.
Erect Norway Maple (*Acer platanoides erectum*) is a good columnar tree and can be used as a screen or accent, or as a street tree. Height, 50 feet. Zone 4.

Fassens Black Maple (*Acer platanoides* 'Fassens Black') with its dark red summer foliage can be used as a lawn specimen. Height, 50 feet. Zone 4.

Globe Norway Maple (*Acer platanoides globosum*) is a small globose tree for restricted sites; may be used as a street tree also. Height, 15 to 20 feet. Zone 4.

Maple, Paperbark (*Acer griseum*). Deciduous. Broad, oval. Rate of growth, moderately slow. Zone 6.

Height. 20 feet.

Leaf and Bark. Three leaflets on a fuzzy stem; medium green. Middle leaflet is 2 to 2½ inches long, half as wide. Old bark peels to show orange-brown color of newer bark.

Culture. Good soil, well drained.

Habitat. Western and central China.

Uses. For a collector's garden.

Comment. The colored bark of older specimens is very striking, especially during the winter and early spring. In foliage and general habit, however, not as good as other small maples. Rare.

Maple, Red (*Acer rubrum*). Deciduous. Semi-oval, irregularly spreading. Rate of growth, rapid. Zone 3.

Height. 75 feet.

Leaf, Flower, Fruit. Leaves are 2½ inches long, 3½ inches wide, 3-lobed; upper surface is medium green, lower surface is light green, and appears silvery as turned by the wind, particularly in early summer. Young leaves are reddish, and in early autumn the mature leaves turn bright red or yellow with red markings. Flowers are red in early April; winged fruits are red in May.

Culture. Tolerant of a variety of soil conditions. Will withstand a poorly drained site better than most trees. Easily transplanted.

Habitat. Eastern and central North America.

Uses. One of the best of the fast-growing trees.

Comment. Not as highly rated as sugar maple. Sometimes called Swamp Maple. The State tree of Rhode Island and national emblem of Canada.

Scanlon Maple (*Acer rubrum conica* 'Scanlon') (Plant Patent 1722), because of its restricted size and neat habit of growth, is more desirable for narrow planting strips. May be used as a street tree. Height 35 feet. Zone 3.

Maple, Silver (*Acer saccharinum*). Deciduous. Irregular, spreading, broad-topped. Several large ascending branches. Open. Rate of growth, rapid. Zone 4*.

Height. 80 feet.

Leaf. Leaves are 5- to 7-lobed, 4 to 6 inches long and about as wide; light green. The mottled yellowish autumn color is not as fine as that of other maples.

Culture. Tolerant although native to moist soils. Readily transplanted. Subject to a variety of leaf insects and particularly to wood-rotting fungi.

Habitat. Eastern United States.

Uses. Temporary lawn tree.

Comment. A fast-growing tree that has been widely used. It has proved to be unsatisfactory as a street tree because its large trunk and buttress roots break walks and curbs, its roots clog service pipes, and its large brittle limbs are readily broken in storms. Sometimes called Soft Maple and *Acer dasycarpum.*

Wiers Weeping Maple (*Acer saccharinum laciniatum*) has more deeply lobed leaves and pendulous branches. Height, 80 feet. Zone 4*.

Maple, Sugar (*Acer saccharum*). Deciduous. Broad, oval. Rate of growth, moderate to slow. Zone 4.

Height. 80 to 100 feet.

Leaf. Leaves are 5 inches long, 5 inches wide, and 5-lobed; light green in spring, changing to medium green, then bright yellow or yellow-orange in the autumn.

Culture. Moderately rich soil. Requires summer moisture but should not be grown on poorly drained site. Prolonged droughts and winter salting of highways weaken or kill this tree. The adverse effects are not immediately noticeable but become evident a year or more later. Transplants readily.

Habitat. Eastern North America.

Uses. Large lawn areas. Along country roads.

Comment. The colorful autumn scenery of the Northeast owes much to this, the State tree of New York, Vermont and Wisconsin.

Black Maple (*Acer nigrum*) is similar and is more commonly seen in the Midwest where it withstands the drier conditions better. Height, 80 feet. Zone 4.

Columnar Sugar Maple (*Acer saccharum columnare*) is a sturdy fastigiate tree with good autumn color. May be used as a street tree. Height, 50 to 70 feet. Zone 4.

Maple, Swamp, see **Maple, Red.**

Maple, Trident (*Acer buergerianum*). Deciduous. Irregular, broad, oval. Outer branches have upward sweep. Rate of growth, moderately rapid. Zone 6.

Height. 25 feet.

Leaf. Leaf is a dark, bright green on upper surface, dull green on lower surface; 2½ inches long and 2 inches wide; 3-lobed, with wedge-shaped base. Foliage turns a dark glistening red in autumn.

Culture. Good, well-drained soil. Fibrous roots; transplants readily. Few pests.

Habitat. Eastern China, Japan.

Uses. At rear corners of property to give variation in height to border planting. Lawn specimen.

Comment. The small dark green leaves of summer and the bright red of autumn recommend this shapely small tree.

Mimosa, see Silk-tree.

Mountain-ash, European (*Sorbus aucuparia*). Deciduous. Oval. Open. Rate of growth, rapid in early years. Zone 3.

Height. 45 feet.

Leaf, Flower, Fruit. Leaves are compound, 5 to 9 inches long, with 6½ pairs of leaflets each of which is 1 to 2½ inches long; bright green, turning yellow-green in autumn. Flowers are white, in clusters 3 to 4 inches across; late May. Fruits, in clusters, are orange to orange-red.

Culture. Well-drained site. Sun. Does poorly when shaded by other trees. Easily transplanted. Trunk borers and leaf-chewing insects may be troublesome.

Habitat. Europe to Siberia.

Uses. Lawn specimen.

Comment. Widely grown. The orange berries are colorful for several weeks in September and early October. Sometimes called Rowan-tree, and in ancient Europe it was thought to keep evil spirits away.

Wilson Columnar Mountain-ash (*Sorbus aucuparia* 'Wilson') is narrowly columnar in form. Height, 35 to 40 feet. Zone 3.

Mountain-ash, Korean (*Sorbus alnifolia*). Deciduous. Conical in younger years; oval at maturity. Dense. Rate of growth, moderately rapid in early years. Zone 4.

Height. 50 feet.

Leaf, Flower, Fruit, Bark. Leaves are 1½ to 4 inches long, ¾ to 1½ inches wide, elliptical, with double-toothed margins; lustrous dark green, turning a clear yellow-orange or scarlet in autumn. Flower clusters are white, up to 5 inches across; individual florets may be 1 inch in diameter; late May. Fruits are scarlet to orange, each being ⅓ to ½ inch long. Bark is smooth and dark gray.

Southern Magnolia is a broad-leaved evergreen with glistening white fragrant flowers. (*Roche*)

The bright orange berries of European Mountain-ash give a dash of color in early autumn. (*Paul E. Genereux*)

Culture.   Tolerant. Few pests.
Habitat.   Central China to Japan.
Uses.   Lawn specimen. Street tree.
Comment.   More shapely than the commonly seen European mountain-ash. Additional advantages are the better foliage color in the autumn and the smooth gray bark for winter interest. Also, it is less subject to borers and leaf-chewing insects.

Mountain-laurel (*Kalmia latifolia*). Broad-leaved evergreen shrub; older specimens may attain stature of a small tree. Dense as a shrub; irregularly round-topped and open at maturity. Rate of growth, slow. Zone 5.
Height.   15 to 30 feet. The larger plants are found in the South.
Leaf and Flower.   Elliptical leaves are 2 to 5 inches long and ¾ to 1½ inches wide; glossy dark green, leathery. Clusters of flowers are 3 to 4 inches across; white, flushed pink, some entirely pink, with dark pink dots, 10-sided; mid-June.
Culture.   Acid, well-drained soil, with humus. Light shade is desirable. Will grow in rather deep shade but blossoms sparsely. Easily moved with ball of soil if root pruned. Lace bug and leaf spot may trouble. It is more rugged than evergreen rhododendrons and its leaves do not curl on cold winter days.
Habitat.   Southern Canada to Georgia, westward to Tennessee, in acid soils. Most abundant in mountain forests.
Uses.   Older specimens, which are open at the base and show irregularly shaped side branches, give an interesting pattern against a wall, or out in the open their silhouettes show to advantage.
Comment.   Its attractive flowers and good foliage are much admired. Sometimes called Calico-bush and, incorrectly, Laurel, which should be reserved for the Laurel or Sweet Bay (*Laurus nobilis*) of Greece from which wreaths for heroes were made. State flower of Connecticut and Pennsylvania.

Nannyberry (*Viburnum lentago*). Deciduous shrub; older specimens may attain stature of a small tree. Irregularly upright. Open. Rate of growth, rapid. Zone 3.
Height.   25 feet.
Leaf, Flower, Fruit.   Leaves are 2 to 4 inches long, half as wide; dark green and glossy, turning purplish red in autumn. Flowers consist of numerous small white florets in flat clusters, 3 to 4 inches across; late May. Fruits are blue-black, oval, ½ inch long.
Culture.   Tolerant of a variety of soils. Will grow in partial shade. Readily transplanted. Few pests.
Habitat.   Eastern United States.

Uses.   Screen. At edge of woodland area.

Comment.   A dependable plant with good foliage. Sometimes called Sheepberry.

Oak, Pin (*Quercus palustris*). Deciduous. Broadly columnar with central leader. Lower branches sweep downward. Numerous short pin-like twigs. Rate of growth, rapid once established. Zone 5.

Height.   70 feet.

Leaf and Fruit.   The deeply lobed leaf is 3 to 5 inches long and nearly as wide, and the 5 to 7 lobes are pointed. It is dark green and glossy, turning bronze to scarlet in autumn. Acorns are about ½ inch long.

Culture.   Moist, rich soil for best growth. Some fibrous roots, therefore is more easily moved than other oaks. Takes a year or two to become established and then grows rapidly. Few pests.

Habitat.   Eastern United States.

Uses.   Lawn specimen where a fast-growing, tough-wooded tree is needed.

Comment.   It has been used as a street tree but the lower branches which sweep downward require constant pruning.

Oak, Pyramidal English (*Quercus robur fastigiata*). Deciduous. Narrow columnar. Secondary branches are fastigiate, paralleling the central stems. Rate of growth, slow. Zone 6.

Height.   60 to 70 feet.

Leaf and Fruit.   Leaves are 2 to 4 inches long, ¾ to 2½ inches wide, with shallow, rounded lobes. No fall color. Acorns are not common on fastigiate form; but on the type they are 1 inch long and there may be two or more to one long stem.

Culture.   Good soil, well drained. Has taproots; move root-pruned plants with a ball of soil. Slow to establish itself. Few pests.

Habitat.   Europe and western Asia.

Uses.   Accent.

Comment.   A tough-wooded plant. One of the better columnar trees but since it is slow growing and difficult to move it is seldom planted. Formerly known as *Quercus pedunculata fastigiata*.

Oak, Red (*Quercus borealis*). Deciduous. Broad, oval, round-topped. Moderately dense. Rate of growth, moderately rapid after becoming established. Zone 4*.

Height.   75 feet.

Leaf and Fruit.   Leaves are 5 to 9 inches long, 4 to 6 inches wide; 7 to 11 lobes, with tapering tips; dark green, turning red in autumn. Acorns are ¾ inch long.

Culture. Tolerant of a variety of soils on well-drained sites. More easily moved than most oaks.

Habitat. Northeastern and central North America.

Uses. Lawn specimen. Street tree.

Comment. The most satisfactory of the commonly planted oaks. Formerly listed as *Quercus rubra.*

Oak, Sawtooth (*Quercus acutissima*). Deciduous. Round-headed, spreading. Moderately dense. Rate of growth, moderately rapid. Zone 6.

Height. 50 feet.

Leaf and Fruit. Leaves are 3 to 6 inches long, 1 to 2¼ inches wide, not lobed, but with sawtooth edge; medium dark green and glossy, remaining green into late fall. Acorns are ¾ to 1¼ inches long.

Culture. Good soil, well drained. Few pests.

Habitat. Japan, Korea, China.

Uses. Lawn specimen. Street tree.

Comment. The best of the medium-sized oaks. Formerly known as *Quercus serrata.*

Oak, Scarlet (*Quercus coccinea*). Deciduous. Broad, oval, round-topped. Dense. Rate of growth, moderate. Zone 4*.

Height. 75 feet.

Leaf and Fruit. Leaves are 3 to 7 inches long, 2½ to 4½ inches wide; 5 to 9 lobes, deeply cut and sharp pointed; bright green and glossy, turning red-bronze to scarlet in autumn. Acorns are ¾ inch long.

Culture. Tolerant. Rather difficult to transplant. Few pests.

Habitat. Eastern and central United States.

Uses. Lawn specimen. Street tree.

Comment. Its glossy leaf provides outstanding fall color, but it is not used as commonly as the red oak, which it resembles.

Oak, Shingle (*Quercus imbricaria*). Deciduous. Round-topped at maturity. Slender branches. Rate of growth, slow. Zone 5.

Height. 60 to 100 feet.

Leaf. Leaves are 4 inches long, 1¾ inches wide; dark green, glossy, elliptical, not lobed; resemble laurel more than the traditional oak. Russet in autumn, turning brown later; held late in season.

Culture. Deep, rich, moist soil. Since it is deep rooted it should be moved in small sizes.

Habitat. Pennsylvania to Georgia, as far west as Nebraska.

Uses. A deep-rooted shade tree that is most compatible with a lawn.

Comment. As with most oaks, it has a strong branch structure that resists storm damage. Since it is an oak that does not look like an oak, it has a special attraction. Sometimes listed as Northern Laurel Oak.

Oak, White (*Quercus alba*). Deciduous. Broad-spreading, rounded crown. Moderately dense. Rate of growth, slow. Zone 4.

Height. 80 feet.

Leaf, Fruit, Bark. Leaves are 5 to 9 inches long, 3 to 6 inches wide; lobes are rounded and rather deeply cut; deep green, muted brownish red in autumn. Acorns are ¾ inch long. Bark is pale gray.

Culture. Well-drained site. One of the most difficult of the oaks to transplant. Slow to become established. Few pests.

Habitat. Eastern United States.

Uses. Large lawn areas, such as parks.

Comment. One of the sturdiest of the oaks because of its exceptionally strong fibers. Long lived. Mature specimens with wide-spreading branches are a memorable sight. State tree of Connecticut and Maryland.

Oak, Willow (*Quercus phellos*). Deciduous. Conical, becoming broadly ovate as it matures. Open. Rate of growth, moderately rapid. Zone 6*.

Height. 50 feet.

Leaf and Fruit. Leaves are 2 to 5 inches long, ⅓ to 1 inch wide; not lobed or toothed; light green and glossy, turning a pale yellow in autumn. Acorns are less than ½ inch long.

Culture. Moist soil; will grow on poorly drained sites. More easily transplanted than most oaks. Few pests.

Habitat. Southeastern United States west to Texas.

Uses. Lawn specimen. Street tree.

Comment. Willow-like leaves give this oak a fine texture. Cannot be used where winters are cold.

Orange, see **Hardy-orange.**

Pagoda-tree, see Alternate-leaf Dogwood under **Dogwood, Flowering;** see also Dogwood, Japanese, and Scholar-tree, Chinese.

Peach, Double White Flowering (*Prunus persica albo-plena*). Deciduous. Broad, spreading top formed by stiff, spreading branches. Open. Rate of growth, rapid. Zone 6.

Height. 20 feet.

Leaf and Flower. Leaves are 3 to 6 inches long, ¾ to 1½ inches wide; medium green, no fall color. Flowers are a glistening white, semi-double, 1½ inches in diameter; late April. Fruit is rarely produced.

Culture. Light, well-drained soil is desirable, but the tree is quite tolerant. Easily transplanted. Few pests, although borers may trouble. (Regular peaches are sprayed to insure healthy fruits.)

Habitat. Species is native to China and has been cultivated since ancient times.

Uses. In an out-of-the-way place but where it will be accessible for picking flowers at time of bloom.

Comment. Short lived and not very shapely. It is admired solely for its flowers. Plants with double pink and red flowers are also available.

Pear, Bradford (*Pyrus calleryana* 'Bradford'). Deciduous. Narrowly conical, becoming broadly oval in shape as it matures. Rate of growth, moderate. Zone 6.

Height. 40 feet.

Leaf, Flower, Fruit. Foliage is dark green and glossy; in late autumn changes to a dark red with lustrous surface which results in a showy display. Clusters of white flowers with lavender stamens in early May. Russet-colored fruit is less than ½ inch long.

Culture. Tolerant of a variety of soil conditions. Resistant to fireblight. Not subject to the usual pear diseases, therefore requires very little spraying.

Habitat. China.

Uses. Specimen. Combined with other trees. Effective in front of taller evergreens.

Comment. The attractive flower, high-quality foliage, and fall color commend this plant to wider use. The small fruits will not litter the lawn. Good branching structure resists wind damage. Similar to Callery pear but is considered superior because it does not develop sharp spur-like growths.

Pea-tree, Siberian (*Caragana arborescens*). Deciduous shrub; older specimens may attain stature of a small tree. Erect, narrow, oval. Rate of growth, moderately rapid. Zone 2.

Height. 15 feet.

Leaf and Flower. Leaf is light green, pinnately compound, 4 inches long; each leaflet is about 1 inch long and ⅝ inch wide. Flowers are yellow, several to a cluster, pea-like; mid-May.

Culture. Tolerant, but prefers sandy loam, sun. Generally free of pests.

Habitat. Siberia.

Uses. Screen. Near buildings where a small upright plant is needed.
Comment. Delicate foliage, extreme hardiness are assets. Sometimes called Pea-shrub.

Pepperidge (*Nyssa sylvatica*). Deciduous. Oval, becoming flat-topped and irregular in areas near the seashore. Rate of growth, moderately slow. Zone 5.
Height. 65 feet.
Leaf and Fruit. Leaves are 2 to 5 inches long, broadly elliptical; dark green and glossy, bright scarlet in autumn. Fruits are about ½ inch long, bluish black, resembling a cherry in shape.
Culture. Quite tolerant. Will grow in poorly drained site. Difficult to transplant, therefore move as a small plant with a ball of soil. Few pests.
Habitat. Maine to Michigan and south to Florida and Texas.
Uses. One of the finest trees for poorly drained sites.
Comment. Brilliant fall color of glossy leaf is outstanding. The difficulty encountered in moving this tree has limited its use. Sometimes known as Tupelo, Black Gum, Sour Gum.

Pine, Austrian (*Pinus nigra*). Needle evergreen. Broad, semi-flat-topped, and somewhat open at maturity. Younger specimens are irregularly upright and dense. Rate of growth, moderately rapid. Zone 4.
Height. 50 to 60 feet.
Leaf and Cone. Needles are 3½ to 6 inches long, in pairs, stiff; dark green. Cones are 2 to 3 inches long.
Culture. Tolerant. Move with ball of soil.
Habitat. Central and southern Europe, Asia Minor.
Uses. Lawn specimen. Windbreak.
Comment. A dark green pine of firm texture. Sometimes known as *Pinus laricio nigricans*.

Pine, Eastern White (*Pinus strobus*). Needle evergreen. Conical when young. Mature specimens may be flat-topped with wide-spreading, horizontal branches. Rate of growth, rapid when young. Zone 3*.
Height. 80 feet.
Leaf. A dark blue-green with slender, flexible needles, 3 to 5 inches long, in bundles of five.
Culture. Will grow in a variety of soils; requires a fair amount of moisture. Has fibrous roots and is one of the most easily moved evergreens. Prune lightly because if heavily pruned into older wood the plant will not send out new growth. Pine weevil may be troublesome.
Habitat. Newfoundland to Georgia, west to Iowa.

Uses. As a single specimen or as a grove. Loses its lower branches as tree grows older, hence it does not have the massivenes of a spruce.

Comment. The needles are soft to the touch and even present an appearance of softness. The aroma of pine needles reminds one of the pure air of northern mountains. State tree of Maine and Minnesota.

Pine, Japanese Black (*Pinus thunbergi*). Needle evergreen. Irregular, somewhat spreading. Rate of growth, slow. Zone 5*.

Height. 40 to 70 feet.

Leaf and Cone. Needles are 2½ to 5 inches long, in pairs, stiff; very dark green. Cones are 1½ to 2½ inches long.

Culture. Well-drained soils. Move with ball of soil. Does well near the seashore.

Habitat. Japan.

Uses. Against the skyline, to emphasize irregular trunk and foliage line.

Comment. A picturesque pine much admired by the Japanese.

Pine, Lace-bark (*Pinus bungeana*). Needle evergreen. Irregularly spreading, flat-topped at maturity. Dense, with exception of older specimens. Rate of growth, slow. Zone 5.

Height. 60 to 70 feet.

Leaf, Cone, Bark. Needles are 3 inches long, three to a bundle, bright green. Cones are 2 to 2½ inches long. Bark of trees that are 30 years or more of age flakes off to show irregular areas of the inner bark which is a creamy white.

Culture. Tolerant of conditions if it is on a well-drained site. Move with a ball of soil. Borers and weevils may be troublesome.

Habitat. Central China.

Uses. Parks. For collectors because of its unusual bark.

Comment. Not as good a shape as most pines. Rarely seen, though the white bark of mature specimens is distinctive.

Pine, Mugo (*Pinus mugo*). Needle evergreen shrub; older specimens may attain stature of a small tree. Irregular outline, broad, spreading. Rate of growth, slow. Zone 3.

Height. 15 to 20 feet.

Leaf and Cone. Needles are 1½ to 3 inches long, in pairs, stiff; dull dark green. Cones are 1 to 2½ inches long.

Culture. Tolerant of a variety of soils. Requires sunlight. Pine needle scale is frequently troublesome.

Habitat. Southern Europe.

Uses. Lawn or garden specimen.

Comment. Small evergreen trees are so rare that tall-growing evergreen shrub selections might be more commonly trained as multi-stemmed specimens. The lower branches should be removed to emphasize the line effect of the several trunks. Formerly known as *Pinus montana.*

Pine, Scotch (*Pinus sylvestris*). Needle evergreen. Broadly columnar and dense as a young tree. Irregular and open, with loss of lower branches, at maturity. Rate of growth, moderately rapid. Zone 3.

Height. 60 to 70 feet.

Leaf, Cone, Bark. Two needles in a bundle, 2 to 3 inches long, flat, twisted; bluish green. Cones are 1½ to 2½ inches long. Upper trunk of mature tree is quite smooth with an orange-brown color.

Culture. Well-drained soil. Sun. Withstands seashore, city, and dry conditions. Transplants readily, but ball of soil is needed if plant is more than a few feet in height. Sawflies and pine scale may bother.

Habitat. Europe, Siberia.

Uses. At the edge of an area it provides an evergreen enframement without much bulk. Silhouette and trunk color are good against open sky.

Comment. Not as massive as most pines. The orange-brown of upper trunk gives a color note which is lacking in other conifers.

Pine, Silver Japanese White (*Pinus parviflora glauca*). Needle evergreen. Horizontal branches of varying lengths. Picturesque. Rate of growth, moderately slow. Zone 6.

Height. 60 feet.

Leaf and Cone. Needles are short, 2 inches. Bluish cast and white line on upper side give a soft gray effect. Cones are only 1½ inches long, remain on tree for six years or more, decorative.

Culture. Will grow in heavy or light soils; good drainage is required.

Habitat. Japan.

Uses. Lawn specimen. Large espalier.

Comment. The foliage color, the decorative cone, and the picturesque shape are assets. By careful pruning, size can be restricted without loss of natural form.

Pine, Swiss Stone (*Pinus cembra*). Needle evergreen. Broad, columnar. Dense. Rate of growth, very slow. Zone 3.

Height. 30 to 40 feet.

Leaf. Needles are 1½ to 4½ inches long, in bundles of five; dark green.

Culture. Tolerant, as long as soil is well drained. To become dense, specimens require good soil. Root-pruned trees develop good root systems. Move with ball of soil. Borers and weevils may attack top stem.

Habitat. Central Europe and northern Asia.

Uses. Screen. Garden specimen.

Comment. Medium-sized evergreen trees are rare, which makes this tree unusual.

Pine, Tanyosho (*Pinus densifolia umbraculifera*). Needle evergreen, Spreading, irregularly flat-topped, usually with several stems. Older specimens are fairly open. Rate of growth, slow. Zone 5.

Height. 15 to 20 feet.

Leaf, Cone, Bark. Needles are in pairs, 2 to 2½ inches long; dark green. Cones are 1½ to 2 inches long. Trunk is reddish and crooked.

Culture. Well-drained, good soil. Move with ball of soil.

Habitat. Japan.

Uses. Lawn or garden specimen.

Comment. A small picturesque pine which with today's smaller gardens deserves to be better known. Also called Umbrella Pine.

Plane, London (*Platanus acerifolia*). Deciduous. Irregularly round-headed. Rate of growth, moderately rapid. Zone 5*.

Height. 75 feet.

Leaf, Fruit, Bark. Leaves are 5 to 10 inches wide, somewhat less in length, 3-lobed; medium light green. Round seed ball is 1 to 1½ inches across, generally in pairs but may be single or in threes, on a pendulous stem. Bark peels off in large flakes to give a mottled effect of buff and greenish gray.

Culture. Tolerant. Few plants better withstand city conditions. Fibrous roots, therefore easily transplanted. At one time it was generally free of pests but canker-stain and other diseases are now considered serious threats.

Habitat. A natural hybrid between American sycamore and Oriental plane.

Uses. Street tree. It has been overplanted, however, which has encouraged disease epidemics.

Comment. Bark is not as light in color as that of American sycamore but it is not so subject to leaf diseases. New York City has used this tree almost exclusively along its streets. Sometimes called Sycamore or Buttonball.

Plum, Purpleleaf, see **Plum, Thundercloud.**

Plum, Thundercloud (*Prunus cerasifera* 'Thundercloud'). Deciduous. Round-headed, with upper branches ascending and middle branches more horizontal. Rate of growth, moderately rapid. Zone 5.

Height. 20 feet.

Leaf, Flower, Fruit. Leaves are up to 2½ inches long and 1¼ inches wide; dark purple from spring until they drop in the autumn. Flower is white, edged with deep pink; late April. Dark-colored fruits are small.

Culture. Tolerant of a variety of soils; withstands drought. Good light is needed to produce the deeper leaf colors. Easily transplanted. Pests are seldom troublesome.

Habitat. Parent plant came from western Asia.

Uses. Near a light-colored building where the dark purple foliage may be desirable.

Comment. Leaf retains purple color in summer better than similar varieties. Flower lasts only a few days but it is early and dependable. The parent plant is sometimes listed as Purpleleaf Plum (*Prunus cerasifera pissardi*).

Poplar, Carolina (*Populus canadensis eugenei*). Deciduous. Broadly columnar, becoming more spreading at maturity. Open. Rate of growth, very rapid. Zone 4*.

Height. 80 feet.

Leaf. Leaves are triangular, 3 to 4 inches long and the same width at the base; medium light green, turning yellow in autumn. Leaf-stalk is long and flattened so that the leaf moves in the slightest breeze.

Culture. Tolerant. Withstands dryness.

Habitat. A hybrid originating in France.

Uses. Temporary lawn tree, but should be removed before it reaches full size.

Comment. Fast growing, short lived, and subject to storm damage. Numerous small branches drop every year. Root system clogs service tiles. It was once widely planted as a street tree but many municipalities have prohibited its use along streets.

Poplar, Japanese (*Populus maximowiczi*). Deciduous. Broad, oval. Open. Rate of growth, very rapid. Zone 5.

Height. 70 feet.

Leaf, Fruit, Bark. Leaves are 3 to 5 inches long, 2½ to 3 inches wide; thick, leathery. Upper surface is dark green and glossy, under surface is light green. Fruiting catkins are 7 to 10 inches long, opening in September to discharge cotton-like seed. Fallen dried catkins show star-shaped patterns. Trunk is light in color.

Culture. Tolerant. Trunk and large branches are subject to canker which permits wood-rotting fungi to enter, shortening the life of the tree.

Habitat. Korea and Japan.

Uses. Temporary tree, to be removed before it reaches full size.

Comment. The large dark green glossy leaf is attractive and contrasts nicely with the light-colored bark.

Poplar, Lombardy (*Populus nigra italica*). Deciduous. Narrow, columnar. Moderately dense. Rate of growth, rapid. Zone 4.

Height.   60 to 70 feet.

Leaf.   Leaf is 2 to 4 inches long and about as wide; generally triangular, broad at base; medium green, light green beneath.

Culture. Tolerant. Easily transplanted. Trunk canker frequently shortens its life.

Habitat. Europe.

Uses. Tall screen. Accent. Use only as a temporary tree.

Comment. The best-known and most widely planted columnar tree. Since it has the many faults of fast-growing trees, it is being supplanted by others of similar shape.

Pride-of-India, see **Goldenrain-tree.**

Privet, Glossy (*Ligustrum lucidum*). Broad-leaved evergreen shrub; older specimens may attain stature of a small tree. Upright, irregularly round-headed. Dense. Rate of growth, rapid in early years. Zone 7*.

Height.   15 to 30 feet.

Leaf, Flower, Fruit.   Leaves are 3 to 5 inches long, 1 to 2 inches wide; dark green, glossy. Flowers are creamy white in 6- to 8-inch clusters in July. Fruits are blue-black, up to ½ inch in diameter, borne on orange stems, in evidence much of the winter.

Culture. Tolerant; withstands drought. Good near the seashore or in the city. Responds well to severe pruning. Few pests, but whitefly bothers in some sections.

Habitat. China, Korea, Japan.

Uses. Lawn specimen. Street tree. Screen. Tub plant. Since it is a heavy feeder it should not be used near a garden.

Comment. Dark green glossy foliage and white flowers add to the attractiveness of this plant. Stately when trained as a tree with a single stem.

Quince, Chinese (*Chaenomeles chinensis*). Deciduous shrub; older specimens may attain stature of a small tree. Broad, columnar. Rate of growth, moderate. Zone 6.

Height.   20 feet.

Leaf, Flower, Bark.   Leaf is dark green, leathery, 2 to 3 inches long and almost as wide. Holds leaves late in season; scarlet color before they fall. Delicate pink flowers, single, 1 to 1½ inches across; early May. Bark flakes off in the manner of a sycamore; mature specimens are colorful.

Culture.   Tolerant of a variety of soil and light conditions but prefers well-drained site. It will not blossom in its northern limit since flower buds are tender.

Habitat.   China.

Uses.   Train as a small tree so that color of trunk can be seen. Espalier.

Comment.   Noteworthy foliage and colorful trunk, yet this plant is very seldom seen.

Redbud, Eastern (*Cercis canadensis*). Deciduous. Branches of varying lengths make pleasantly irregular crown. The effect of a multi-stemmed tree is obtained if lower side branches are retained. Rate of growth, moderate. Zone 5*.

Height.   25 feet.

Leaf, Flower, Bark.   Leaves are light green, round, 3 to 5 inches. Magenta flowers, small but in great number in mid-May, appear on both young and old wood, including the upper portion of the trunk. Stems are dark in color, somewhat irregular.

Culture.   Moderately rich soil with good drainage. Few fibrous roots, therefore difficult to transplant. Start with small balled-and-burlapped plants; spring planting advised. May be slow to become established, but it is more winter hardy than many give it credit for.

Habitat.   New Jersey to Missouri and southward.

Uses.   Good near a garden since it takes little nutriment from upper layer of soil.

Comment. The State tree of Oklahoma. Effective spring flowers and winter silhouette. Sometimes called Judas-tree.

Wither's Pink Charm and Pinkbud are recent selections that are considered more desirable than the magenta color of the type. For both, height, 25 feet. Zone 5*.

White Redbud (*Cercis canadensis alba*) was found sometime before 1900 in Missouri. It is now being grown by a few nurserymen and because of its color is preferred by many people. Height, 25 feet. Zone 5*.

Red-cedar (*Juniperus virginiana*). Needle evergreen. Broad, columnar. Generally dense. Rate of growth, moderately rapid. Zone 3.

Height.   30 to 50 feet.

Leaf, Fruit, Bark. Needles are dark green, small, flat, overlapping, and appressed. Most twigs have some short pointed needles at an acute angle, known as juvenile foliage. Fruit is round, berry-like, dark blue. Bark is reddish brown, peeling in long, loose strips.

Culture. Well-drained soil, full sun. Not easily transplanted, therefore nursery-grown balled-and-burlapped plants should be selected for spring planting. Pests include bagworm and red spider.

Habitat. Canada to Florida and west to Rocky Mountains.

Uses. Background for garden features. Accent.

Comment. The State tree of Tennessee. Native plants vary in their degree of compactness, and they frequently take on a brownish cast during the colder months. Horticultural selections have been made with the idea of producing uniformly good specimens. Two of these are:

Canaert (*Juniperus virginiana canaerti*), dark green all year, heavy fruiting. Height, 30 feet. Zone 3.

Burk (*Juniperus virginiana burki*), gray-green foliage turning purplish in winter. Height, 20 feet. Zone 3.

Rhododendron, Rosebay (*Rhododendron maximum*). Broad-leaved evergreen shrub; older specimens may attain stature of a small tree. Round-topped and dense to the ground if grown in the open. Rate of growth, moderately slow. Zone 4.

Height. 15 feet; 30 feet in the South.

Leaf and Flower. Leaf is dark green, 5 to 8 inches long, 1 to 2½ inches wide. At 20 degrees above zero the leaves start to roll and as the temperature falls they roll tighter and may become pencil-thin. As the temperature moderates, the leaves open out again. Flowers are 1½ inches across, white with a blush of pink; stamens are pale lavender; early July.

Culture. Acid soil, good loam rich in humus with ample moisture in the summer and late autumn. Move with ball of soil. Shallow rooted; mulch with oak leaves or peatmoss. Pests include lace bug and black vine weevil.

Habitat. Nova Scotia to Georgia.

Uses. Screen.

Comment. One of the hardiest broad-leaved evergreens. The State flower of West Virginia. Since foliage is coarse it should not be used near refined architectural features.

Rose-of-Sharon (*Hibiscus syriacus*). Deciduous shrub; older specimens may attain stature of a small tree. Stiffly erect with many ascending branches. Rate of growth, moderately slow. Zone 5*.

Height. 15 feet.

Leaf and Flower. Leaf is deep green, semi-lobed, coarsely round-toothed, 2½ inches long, 2 inches wide; late to appear in spring; long lasting in autumn. Flowers are 2½ to 4 inches across, white, pink, red, blue, or white with red eye; mostly single, some double; August.

Culture. Tolerant of a variety of soil conditions. Will grow well in a city or near the seashore. For best flowers, prune back previous year's growth to three buds in late winter.

Habitat. China and India.

Uses. As a screen.

Comment. Late summer flowers are its chief asset. White-flowered variety recommended since the blues and some of the pinks turn a dull magenta-purple as they fade. Sometimes called Shrub Althea.

Rowan-tree, see **Mountain-ash, European.**

Russian-olive (*Elaeagnus angustifolia*). Deciduous. Broad, irregularly rounded, often retaining lower branches. Rate of growth, moderately rapid in early years. Zone 3.

Height. 20 to 25 feet.

Leaf, Flower, Fruit, Bark. Leaves are 1 to 3 inches long and about ½ inch wide; dull gray-green on upper surface, silvery underneath; held late with little change of color. Small flowers are yellowish, rather inconspicuous but fragrant. Small oblong fruit is silver flushed with rose. Old bark is dark in color, furrowed, and may have knobby irregular growths.

Culture. Very tolerant; withstands drought. Does well near the seashore. Accepts pruning well, and some is needed to remove dead twigs. Easily moved because of its fibrous roots. Pests are not common, but aphids are troublesome in some places.

Habitat. Southern Europe and central Asia.

Uses. For color contrast or in adverse conditions where other plants do not thrive.

Comment. The light gray foliage is distinctive. The irregular, twisted trunk of older specimens lends character.

Scholar-tree, Chinese (*Sophora japonica*). Deciduous. Broad, oval. Dense in early years, becoming moderately open. Rate of growth, moderate. Zone 5*.

Height. 40 to 60 feet.

Leaf, Flower, Fruit, Bark. Compound leaves are 6 to 10 inches long, with 9 to 15 leaflets each 1 to 2 inches long and half as wide; dark green and held late with no change of color. Seed is in green, constricted bean pod. Small twigs and even three- and four-year-old branches are green. Flowers are cream colored, arranged in large clusters. Blooms in early August, for an extended period.

Culture. Quite tolerant of a variety of soil conditions. Withstands drought and city conditions. Transplants readily but should be moved with a ball of soil. Pests are rarely troublesome.

Habitat. China and Korea. Has long been cultivated in Japan.

Uses. Lawn specimen. Street tree. Can be used near gardens since few trees are as compatible with flowers and vegetables.

Comment. Fine-textured tree with interest from summer flowers. Seed pods remain green even after leaves have fallen, and combined with green twigs give color in early winter. Although young trees do not flower, this is a plant of high quality which deserves to be used more freely. Sometimes called Japanese Pagoda-tree.

Sea-buckthorn (*Hippophaë rhamnoides*). Deciduous shrub; older specimens may attain stature of a small tree. Irregularly rounded. Open. Rate of growth, moderate. Zone 3*.

Height. 15 to 25 feet.

Leaf, Flower, Fruit. Leaves are 1 to 3 inches long, no more than ¼ inch wide; dark grayish green on upper surface, silvery gray beneath. Male and female flowers are on separate plants. Fruit is ¼ inch in diameter, orange color in autumn, and persists into the winter.

Culture. Tolerant of a variety of soil conditions; prefers well-drained site; is at its best in non-acid soils. Does well near the seashore. Fibrous roots. Sends up suckers which may be troublesome.

Habitat. Europe and Asia.

Uses. Screen.

Comment. The narrow gray foliage and the long-lasting orange berries are assets, especially in seaside gardens.

Serviceberry, see **Shadblow.**

Shadblow, Allegheny (*Amelanchier laevis*). Deciduous. Taller than wide; irregular outline. Quite open. Rate of growth, moderately rapid. Zone 4.

Height. 30 feet.

Leaf, Flower, Fruit, Bark. Light green leaf is of medium-fine texture, 1½ to 2½ inches long and somewhat more than half as wide. Unfolding leaf is purple-bronze; fall color is yellowish. Drooping clusters of white flowers; late April. Red to black fruits in early summer; favorite of birds. Trunk is smooth and gray.

Culture. Tolerant of a variety of soil conditions. Does best in partial shade. Easily transplanted. Belongs to the same family as the apple and is subject to some of the same leaf diseases, such as cedar rust.

Habitat. Eastern United States.

Uses. At edge of woodland. Near evergreens to lighten their massive effect.

Comment. Flowers contrast nicely with purple-bronze color of new foliage. Gray trunk of multi-stemmed plant is highly rated. Sometimes called Serviceberry or Shadbush.

The similar and more common but less showy Downy Shadblow (*Amelanchier canadensis*) has unfolding leaves covered with grayish hairs. Height, 30 feet. Zone 4.

Sheepberry, see **Nannyberry.**

Shrub Althea, see **Rose-of-Sharon.**

Silk-tree (*Albizzia julibrissin*). Deciduous. Flat-topped, spreading. Fine-textured tropical appearance. Rate of growth, moderate. Zone 7.

Height. 20 feet.

Leaf and Flower. Doubly compound leaf is 9 to 18 inches long and half as wide; 20 to 30 pairs of leaflets, each about ½ inch long and ⅛ inch wide. Leaves drop at the first frost. The white to pink powder-puff flowerheads are attractive from July to September; the numerous long stamens rather than the usual petals make up the showy part of the flower.

Culture. Good, well-drained soil is necessary. Withstands heat and drought. Move with a ball of soil and only in the spring. When grown in the North, the trunk of even the hardy strain should be protected from sun scald either with a burlap wrap or by using an anti-desiccant spray.

Habitat. Iran to central China.

Uses. Near a large garden or at rear edge of property.

Comment. The large, fern-like leaves provide a tropical effect. The long-lasting flowering season is an asset. Although silk-tree is frequently called Mimosa, that name should be reserved for species of *Acacia,* which are tender plants.

Hardy Silk-tree (*Albizzia julibrissin rosea*) has a deeper pink color than the type. Height, 20 feet. Zone 6.

Silverbell, Carolina (*Halesia carolina*). Deciduous. Irregularly upright. Moderately dense. Rate of growth, slow. Zone 5.

Height. 20 to 30 feet.

Leaf, Flower, Fruit. Leaves are 2 to 5 inches long and about half as wide; medium green, turning to dull yellow in autumn. Flowers are

Japanese Black Pine is admired for its picturesque habit of growth. (*Paul E. Genereux*)

Silk-tree has a uniquely shaped flower. The delicate pink blossoms are displayed for several weeks during the summer.
(*Roche*)

white, ½ to 1 inch long, bell-shaped; mid-May. Fruit is about 1 inch long and has four wings.

Culture. Rich, well-drained soil. Fibrous rooted, nevertheless it is best moved with a ball of soil. Few pests.

Habitat. Southeastern United States.

Uses. As a screen, or at corners of property.

Comment. The most commonly planted silverbell. Not as large in any way as Mountain Silverbell. Formerly known as *Halesia tetraptera.*

Silverbell, Mountain (*Halesia monticola*). Deciduous. Taller than wide, with main branches of ascending habit and short secondary branches of horizontal habit. Rate of growth, moderately rapid. Zone 5*.

Height. 40 to 50 feet.

Leaf, Flower, Fruit. Leaves are 5 inches long and about half as wide; medium to light green with little, if any, fall color. White bell-like flowers arranged along the twigs are up to 2 inches long; mid-May. The dry fruits with four fins as appendages are almost 2 inches long.

Culture. Quite tolerant if soil is well drained. Move with a ball of soil. Sometimes slow to become established. Pests seldom trouble, but any trunk wounds should be painted to prevent attack by wood-rotting fungi.

Habitat. Mountains of Tennessee and Georgia.

Uses. Lawn specimen. Street tree.

Comment. This is one of the few medium-sized trees with showy flowers. Rarely seen.

Smoke-tree, American (*Cotinus americanus*). Deciduous shrub; older specimens may attain stature of a small tree. Round-headed, oval, regular in outline. Fairly dense. Rate of growth, slow. Zone 6.

Height. 25 feet.

Leaf and Fruit. Leaf is 2 to 4 inches long and 1½ to 3 inches wide; brilliant scarlet to orange in the autumn. Fruiting panicles are small and sparse.

Culture. Well-drained loam. Fibrous roots.

Habitat. Tennessee to Texas.

Uses. Lawn specimen. Street tree.

Comment. Trunk may be as much as 1 foot in diameter. A tree of orderly habit with outstanding fall color. Rarely seen. Formerly known as *Rhus cotinoides* and sometimes known as Chittam-wood.

Smoke-bush (*Cotinus coggygria*), a European relative, has been widely planted for the smoke effect of its seed pods during the summer. Height, 15 feet. Zone 6.

Snowbell, Japanese (*Styrax japonica*). Deciduous. Irregularly spreading, with slender branches. Open. Rate of growth, moderate. Zone 6.
Height. 20 feet.
Leaf and Flower. Leaves are 1 to 3½ inches long and half as wide; glossy dark green. Flowers are white, reflexed bells, 1 to 1½ inches long, with a half dozen spaced along a single stalk; early June.
Culture. Light soil with humus added; well drained. Few pests.
Habitat. China and Japan.
Uses. Lawn or garden specimen.
Comment. A graceful flowering tree that is rarely seen.

Sorrel-tree (*Oxydendrum arboreum*). Deciduous. Upright, narrow, oval. Slender trunk. Open. Rate of growth, moderately slow. Zone 5.
Height. 25 feet.
Leaf, Flower, Fruit. Leaves are rather narrow and 5 to 7 inches long; lustrous, leathery; dark green on upper surface; brilliant scarlet in October. White flowers in 6- to 10-inch horizontal racemes appear in mid-July. The creamy seed capsules contrast with fall foliage.
Culture. Acid soil with some humus. Belongs to the same group as the rhododendron and is the most tree-like member of the Heath family. Will withstand some shade but the best fall color occurs in full sun. Pests seldom bother.
Habitat. Pennsylvania to Florida, west to Indiana and Louisiana. Common in the Blue Ridge Mountains.
Uses. Specimen. At edge of woods; near a shrub border to give height; or near rhododendrons and azaleas since it is of the same family.
Comment. The summer flowers, the glossy summer foliage, and the showy autumn color help to make this a choice plant. Sometimes called Sourwood, and in some advertisements is listed as Lily-of-the-valley-tree.

Sourwood, see Sorrel-tree.

Spindle-tree, European (*Euonymus europaeus*). Deciduous shrub; older specimens may attain stature of a small tree. Oval. Moderately dense, becoming open with age. Rate of growth, moderate. Zone 4*.
Height. 15 to 20 feet.
Leaf and Fruit. Leaves are 1 to 3 inches long and about half as wide; dull dark green, held late, usually with no change of color. Fruit is reddish purple, opens to show orange-colored seed.
Culture. Very tolerant. Numerous fibrous roots; readily trans-

planted. Aphids sometimes are so numerous as to curl leaves and make control difficult.

Habitat. Europe to western Asia.

Uses. Screen.

Comment. Outstanding display of fruit. Its relationship to bitter-sweet is clearly shown in its fruit formation although the color is a reddish purple instead of orange. Sometimes called Bursting Heart. Formerly listed as *Euonymus europaea*.

Spruce, Colorado (*Picea pungens*). Needle evergreen. Conical. Dense. Rate of growth, slow. Zone 3.

Height. 50 to 70 feet.

Leaf and Cone. Needles are ¾ to 1¼ inches long, sharp pointed; dark green. Cones are 3 to 4 inches long and pendent.

Culture. Rich, moist soil. Full sun. Move with ball of soil. Spruce gall aphid and red spider may be troublesome.

Habitat. Mountains of Colorado, Wyoming, Utah, and Arizona.

Uses. Specimen. As a clump for large lawn areas only.

Comment. The tree appears amiss if lower branches are removed. Requires considerable space so it is out of place on small properties. The State tree of Colorado and Utah.

Colorado Blue Spruce (*Picea pungens glauca*) has needles of steel blue color. Height, 50 to 70 feet. Zone 3.

Spruce, Norway (*Picea abies*). Needle evergreen. Conical. Rate of growth, moderately rapid. Zone 3.

Height. 75 feet.

Leaf. Needles are ½ to ¾ inch long, medium dark green. Mature specimens display small pendulous branchlets, giving a less severe form than that of other spruces.

Culture. Will grow in a variety of soils but requires moisture. Does not like city conditions. To retain a good form, it needs light and the cooler and more moist summers of higher elevations. Withstands wind much better than hemlock. It has a fibrous root system but, as is true of all evergreens, it should be moved with a ball of soil. Spruce gall aphid may appear.

Habitat. Northern and central Europe. Has long been in cultivation and was used in Colonial days.

Uses. Wide-spreading branches sweeping the ground are a most effective windbreak.

Comment. Not for the small property. A sad sight is a pair of these trees used in front of a small house with an entrance walk trying to find its way through the low sweeping branches.

Stewartia, Korean (*Stewartia koreana*). Deciduous. Broad, oval. Rate of growth, moderately slow. Zone 6.

Height. 35 feet.

Leaf, Flower, Bark. Leaf is medium green, 3 inches long, 1¾ inches wide. Unusual fall color, orange-red areas of varying intensity speckled with dark spots. Flower is white, 3 inches in diameter; July. Trunk is smooth with color blotches of light browns, dark grays, and pale greens.

Culture. Good soil with humus; acid, ample moisture. Should not be exposed to strong winter winds.

Habitat. Korea.

Uses. Lawn specimen. Attractive in a garden setting.

Comment. The mottled bark should be considered the prime interest, with the summer flower and fall color as worthy bonuses. Sometimes called False Camellia.

Sweet-gum (*Liquidambar styraciflua*). Deciduous. Younger trees are conical with central leader; mature specimens have large, wide-spreading branches. Rate of growth, moderately slow. Zone 6.

Height. 70 to 90 feet.

Leaf, Fruit, Bark. Leaves are 4 to 7 inches wide and almost as long, 5- to 7-lobed. Lustrous deep green, changing in late fall to a mosaic of colors. A single plant may have deep red, crimson, yellow, and bronze tones. Fruit is a globose head made up of beaked capsules, 1 to 1½ inches in diameter. Younger branches may have conspicuous corky ridges.

Culture. Tolerant, but does not like a dry site. Since it has a taproot it is difficult to move, particularly in larger sizes. Move with ball of soil. Few pests.

Habitat. Southern Connecticut to Florida and west to Missouri and parts of Mexico.

Uses. Lawn specimen. Street tree for wide planting strips.

Comment. Star-shaped leaf somewhat resembles a maple but it has an unusually clean-cut effect. Horizontal branching habit is structurally more sound than the sharp-angle branching of the maple. The late autumn color is very striking.

Sycamore, see **Plane, London.**

Tulip-tree (*Liriodendron tulipifera*). Deciduous. Cylindrical. Tall, erect, with a straight trunk. Rate of growth, moderately rapid in early years. Zone 5.

Height.   90 feet.

Leaf and Flower.   Leaves are 2½ to 5 inches long and 3 to 6 inches wide with a broad, shallow notch at the apex; golden yellow in early autumn. Flowers are greenish yellow with an orange spot at the base, 2 inches in diameter; mid-June. Does not flower until it is about 20 years old.

Culture.   Deep, well-drained soil. Transplants with difficulty. Plant small trees, in the spring only, and with a ball of soil.

Habitat.   Massachusetts to Mississippi and west to Arkansas.

Uses.   Large park areas, because of its great height.

Comment.   High-branched mature specimens are stately. Unique flower and leaf set this tree apart. Pattern of leaf resembles stylized tulip blossom and the flower also bears some resemblance to the tulip. Sometimes called Whitewood and Tulip Poplar. The State tree of Indiana and Kentucky.

Tupelo, see **Pepperidge.**

Umbrella-pine   (*Sciadopitys verticillata*). Needle evergreen. Broad, columnar. Normally retains lower branches. Dense. Rate of growth, slow. Zone 6.

Height.   30 feet. A 100-foot specimen may be seen in Japan.

Leaf.   Needles are 3 to 5 inches long, dark green and glossy. Some 20 to 30 are arranged in a whorl not dissimilar to the ribs of an umbrella that has blown inside out.

Culture.   Good, well-drained soil. At its best in coastal sections and will even withstand a considerable amount of salt spray. Pests are few.

Habitat.   Central Japan.

Uses.   A distinctive specimen. Since it is slow growing, it can be used as a tub plant. If used in this way in areas where the soil in the container would freeze solid, the plant may be removed and planted in a row garden for the colder months.

Comment.   It is unique in appearance and it is admired by the most discriminating. Its glossy needles are unlike those of any other evergreen.

Viburnum, Blackhaw   (*Viburnum prunifolium*). Deciduous shrub; older specimens may attain stature of a small tree. Irregular outline; some short stout branches give a rugged appearance. Rate of growth, moderately slow. Zone 3*.

Height.   15 to 20 feet.

The dainty shape of the Japanese Snowbell blossoms attracts attention in late spring. (*Roche*)

Sorrel-tree has long clusters of flowers in the summer. Its glossy leaves turn a bright red in the autumn. (*Paul E. Genereux*)

Leaf, Flower, Fruit. Leaves are dark green, semi-glossy, 2½ inches long, 1½ inches wide (smaller than other viburnums); dark plum-red in autumn. Cluster of white flowers, 2 to 4 inches across; mid-May. Blue-black berries are ½ inch long.

Culture. Tolerant of a variety of soil and light conditions. Withstands drought. Readily transplanted. Seldom troubled by pests.

Habitat. Connecticut to Georgia, west to Arkansas.

Uses. Screen. Espalier; strong horizontal branches require little or no support.

Comment. Good foliage which even during prolonged dry spells looks fresh while nearby plants appear dingy. Large flower cluster is attractive.

Viburnum, Siebold (*Viburnum sieboldi*). Deciduous shrub; older specimens may attain stature of a small tree. Older plants are not as wide as they are high. Rate of growth, moderately rapid. Zone 5.

Height. 15 to 20 feet.

Leaf, Flower, Fruit. Leaves are light green, deeply veined, semi-glossy, up to 5 inches long, 1½ to 3 inches wide; held late with little change of color. Flowers are in stalked cluster, white, 3 to 4 inches across; late May. Fruit is bright red in late summer, later turns black and drops; each fruit stands out individually on a rather stout red stem.

Culture. Tolerant except for extreme dryness. Easily transplanted. Seldom troubled by pests.

Habitat. Japan.

Uses. Screen.

Comment. Fruit cluster is outstanding; foliage is distinctive.

Whitewood, see **Tulip-tree.**

Willow, Babylon Weeping (*Salix babylonica*). Deciduous. Fountain-like with long, slender pendulous branches that sway in the breeze. Rate of growth, rapid. Zone 5.

Height. 40 feet.

Leaf and Flower. Leaves are 3 to 5 inches long, ½ inch wide. Yellow-green in early spring, then medium green above and light green underneath, and yellow in autumn.

Culture. Quite tolerant, but does not thrive on poor, dry soils. Easily transplanted. Cankers on trunk can kill the tree within a few years; no control. Borers and leaf insects may be troublesome.

Habitat. China.

Uses. At edge of lake. In a city garden where other trees might be poor risks.

Comment. The weeping willow is graceful and with its slender twigs and narrow foliage is delicate in pattern. Where space permits, a grouping of several can be most pleasing.

The Japanese have sometimes used this tree to good effect by training the trunk to an irregular line, then drastically pruning the crown to restrict its size and to keep the foliage sparse enough to reveal the crooked trunk.

The several shortcomings of the willow must be recognized. It is naturally short lived, and the insects and diseases to which it is so subject make its life tenure uncertain. Branches are easily broken by sleet and wind; its roots are notorious water seekers, clogging wells, drains, and other service tiles. Where the property is of such a size that only a few trees can be used, it would be inadvisable to select the willow.

Golden Weeping Willow (*Salix alba tristis*) has yellow twigs and is one of the more hardy willows. It is sometimes confused in the trade with Babylon Weeping Willow. Height, 40 feet. Zone 4.

Ringleaf Willow (*Salix babylonica crispa*) has a leaf that is twisted like a ram's horn. Height, 40 feet. Zone 5.

Willow, Contorted Hankow (*Salix matsudana tortuosa*). Deciduous. Irregular, narrow, oval. Up-sweeping branches. Open. Rate of growth, rapid. Zone 5.

Height. 40 feet.

Leaf. Leaves are 2 to 4 inches long, less than ½ inch wide; bright green turning dull yellow in autumn. Twigs and even older branches are twisted or contorted.

Culture. Tolerant; will grow on poorly drained sites. Withstands city conditions. Easily transplanted. Subject to the usual pests of willows.

Habitat. Species is native to northern China and Korea.

Uses. Temporary tree of medium size and unusual winter lines for a light screen.

Comment. Twisted stems offer an interesting willow silhouette against a high wall or against the sky. Sometimes called Corkscrew Willow.

Yellow-wood (*Cladrastis lutea*). Deciduous. Broadly rounded, fairly open. Rate of growth, moderate. Zone 5*.

Height. 45 feet.

Leaf, Flower, Fruit, Bark. Compound leaves are 8 to 12 inches long, with 7 to 11 leaflets, each of which is 3 to 4 inches long; medium light green, yellow in autumn. White flowers in mid-June appear in long wisteria-like clusters. Usually flowers heavily in alternate years.

Seeds are in long, thin bean pods, turning brown and persisting for
months. Bark is smooth and gray.

Culture. Moderately rich soil for good growth. It will also grow in
soil that is only fair since it is a legume and makes its own nitrogen.
Well-drained site. Wood is brittle but is rarely broken by ice or winds.
Insects and diseases are rarely troublesome.

Habitat. Tennessee, Kentucky, North Carolina.

Uses. Lawn specimen. Occasionally as a street tree.

Comment. One of the showiest in flower of the larger trees. Gray
bark adds interest. The bark was once used as a dye for homespun
cloth.

Yew, Upright, Japanese (*Taxus cuspidata capitata*). Needle evergreen
shrub; older specimens may attain stature of a small tree. Upright,
with a single leader. Rate of growth, slow. Zone 5.

Height. 25 to 30 feet.

Leaf. Needles are dark green but not as dark as some selected
clones of the more dwarf varieties. Growth is not as dense as most
yews although annual shearing will overcome this.

Culture. Tolerant of a variety of soils but prefers a good one
that is well drained and not too acid. Excessive watering on heavy soil
or too deep planting is fatal. Will grow in sun or partial shade.
Nursery-grown plants that have been root pruned transplant well.
Move with a ball of soil in the spring, summer, or fall. Few plants
accept pruning better, and if compactness is desired pruning should be
done as new growth develops in early summer. More so than any
other common conifer, it will send out new growth from older branches
that are headed back. Withstands city conditions better than other
conifers. Generally free of pests but black vine weevil and a soft scale
may appear.

Habitat. Japan.

Uses. At the end of a fence or near a corner to give height. As a
small grove.

Comment. Small, needle evergreen trees are a rarity, yet there are
many needs for such a plant. If some of the lower branches are removed, the reddish, shredding bark is revealed as an extra note of
interest.

Zelkova (*Zelkova serrata*). Deciduous. Broad, round-topped, with
ascending branches. Not dense. Rate of growth, moderate. Zone 5*.

Height. 80 feet.

Leaf, Fruit, Bark. Leaves are 1 to 3 inches long, ¾ to 2 inches
wide; deep green, changing to a russet red in the autumn. Fruits are

round, ⅛ inch in diameter. Twigs are fine, giving a good winter silhouette. Trunk of mature tree is smooth and gray, and flakes off to show irregular areas of pale green and tan.

Culture. Tolerant, but best on good soils with ample moisture. Fibrous root system, therefore easily transplanted.

Habitat. Japan.

Uses. Lawn specimen. Street tree.

Comment. It is related to the elms but shows resistance to the pests that beset the elm. It has a smaller leaf and better autumn color than the American elm. The bark of mature specimens is outstanding. Sometimes called Japanese Keaki and Gray-barked Elm.

CHAPTER 16

Fifty Additional Trees with Comments

The trees listed in this chapter fall into several categories: (1) Natives that are well known to many but are not adapted to most present-day plantings; (2) plants of limited usage for special sites; (3) trees that once were widely planted but are not well rated by today's standards; (4) trees that have been grown only in a few collections and therefore need further trial and evaluation; and (5) trees that are difficult to obtain because of their rarity in the trade.

Many of the trees in this list have excellent qualities, and where healthy specimens exist they certainly should be retained unless they are crowding out more desirable species. One of the favorite trees near my home is a multiple-stemmed yellow birch 13 feet in circumference which was mature at the time the property was purchased some 27 years ago. I should be unhappy to lose it for any reason, and I have even gone to the expense of putting in several cables to prevent the possibility of any of its several trunks splitting off. To me, this is a first-rate tree, even though I would classify the species only in a secondary list.

Apple (*Malus pumila*). The twisted trunk and irregular shape of older specimens can be picturesque. Flowers are admired but the fruit, unless constantly sprayed, is considered a nuisance. Height, 40 feet. Zone 3.

Ash, Flowering (*Fraxinus ornus*). Dense crown of dark green foliage. Abundant white flowers, fragrant. Height, 35 feet. Zone 6.

Ash, Green (*Fraxinus pennsylvanica lanceolata*). Bright, shiny green foliage. Seedlings are troublesome. Marshall seedless ash is an improved form. Height, 60 feet. Zone 3.

Ash, White (*Fraxinus americana*). Compound leaves of 7 or 9 oval leaflets are dull green, turn deep purple in autumn. Die-back disease may occur. Height, 90 feet. Zone 4.

Bald-cypress (*Taxodium distichum*). Non-evergreen conifer. Fine needles are attractive in summer. Hardy in the North although native to the South. Height, 60 feet. Zone 5.

Birch, Black (*Betula lenta*). Black color of trunk contrasts with other trees. Inner bark of twig has a wintergreen flavor. Sometimes called Sweet Birch. Height, 75 feet. Zone 4*.

Birch, River (*Betula nigra*). Light reddish-brown bark peels off in thin layers; most evident on 4- to 6-inch trunks. Height, 80 feet. Zone 5.

Birch, Yellow (*Betula lutea*). Silvery yellowish-gray bark peels in thin ribbon-like layers. Prefers a woodsy setting. Height, 70 feet. Zone 3.

Cedar-of-Lebanon (*Cedrus libani*). Evergreen. Famous old trees can be found in the Holy Land. A hardy strain has been found which does well in Boston. Height, 70 feet. Zone 6.

Cherry, European Bird (*Prunus padus*). One of the first trees to leaf out. Long clusters of fragrant white flowers in early May. Numerous small black fruits. Height, 40 feet. Zone 3*.

Cherry, Red-bark (*Prunus serrula*). Dark reddish-brown bark is glossy. It is especially noteworthy during the winter months. Height, 20 feet. Zone 6.

Coffee-tree, Kentucky (*Gymnocladus dioicus*). No small twigs; therefore tree presents a rugged appearance in winter. Provides light shade. Height, 80 feet. Zone 4*.

Dove-tree (*Davidia involucrata*). Large white flowers of odd shape in mid-May are individually spectacular, but tree does not flower freely. Large leaves turn yellow in autumn. Height, 30 feet. Zone 6*.

Elm, English (*Ulmus procera*). Round-headed stately tree that does well in cities. Subject to the many insects and diseases that plague most elms. Height, 90 feet. Zone 6.

Evodia, Korean (*Evodia danielli*). Dark green compound leaves; white flowers in a cluster, mid-August; red husks open to display small glossy black seed. Height, 25 feet. Zone 6.

False-cypress, Sawara (*Chamaecyparis pisifera*). Evergreen. Fast growing, but less attractive at maturity than most evergreens. Best used as a tall screen. Tightly sheared specimens once commonly seen in foundation plantings. Height, 60 feet. Zone 5.

Filbert, Turkish (*Corylus colurna*). Dark green leaves; rather dense, stately form. Remains a good green when other trees suffer from drought. Height, 50 feet. Zone 5.

Fir, Nikko (*Abies homolepis*). Vigorous evergreen with slender 4-inch cones. Needles are dark green above, whitish on underside. Makes a good specimen. Height, 70 feet. Zone 5.

Fir, Southern Balsam (*Abies fraseri*). Conical evergreen. Can be used in place of balsam fir, which will not stand summers south of Zone 2. Good for Christmas trees. Height, 70 feet. Zone 5.

Hackberry (*Celtis occidentalis*). A rugged tree that grows quite rapidly. Withstands dryness and cold. Height, 75 feet. Zone 3.

Horse-chestnut (*Aesculus hippocastanum*). Stately oval form. Large clusters of whitish flowers in mid-May. Disadvantages: coarse foliage, subject to leaf blight in wet weather and leaf scorch if season is very dry; litter created by woody fruits. Height, 70 feet. Zone 3*.

Horse-chestnut, Ruby (*Aesculus carnea brioti*). Large red flower clusters attract attention. No fruit to produce litter. Height, 60 feet. Zone 4.

Incense-cedar (*Libocedrus decurrens*). Broad columnar evergreen. Resembles an arborvitae but is less hardy. Height, 70 feet. Zone 6.

Larch, European (*Larix decidua*). Non-evergreen conifer with better growth habit than American species. Once commonly planted in parks. Height, 80 feet. Zone 3.

Larch, Golden (*Pseudolarix amabilis*). Non-evergreen conifer. Foliage resembles larch but needle is wider and better arranged. Strong horizontal branches give distinction. Striking golden color in the autumn. Height, 70 feet. Zone 6.

Linden, American (*Tilia americana*). Not as shapely or as long lived as the more widely planted European lindens. Fragrant flowers. Sometimes called Basswood. Height, 75 feet. Zone 4.

Locust, Black (*Robinia pseudoacacia*). White flowers in pendulous clusters are fragrant. A durable wood that resists rot. Leaf miner attacks foliage; borers are commonly found in trunk. Height, 65 feet. Zone 4.

Magnolia, Bigleaf (*Magnolia macrophylla*). The largest leaf of any of the deciduous magnolias. Leaves may be 30 inches long, 10 inches wide, flowers a foot across. Height, 50 feet. Zone 7.

Maple, Amur (*Acer ginnala*). Same size as Japanese maple but hardier. When grown on well-drained site, leaf turns yellow, then bright scarlet in autumn. Height, 20 feet. Zone 3.

Maple, Painted (*Acer mono*). A maple of medium size is a rarity; this one deserves to be more widely tried, but is difficult to purchase. Foliage yellow in autumn. Height, 50 feet. Zone 6.

Maple, Striped (*Acer pensylvanicum*). Smooth bark, reddish brown or dark green with vertical white streaks. Winged seeds in a long cluster. Good understory tree in woodland. Height, 25 feet. Zone 4*.

Maple, Sycamore (*Acer pseudoplatanus*). Wide-spreading tree of vigorous growth. Large leaf resembles that of sycamore. Winged seeds in a pendulous cluster. Does well near seashore. Height, 60 feet. Zone 5.

Mulberry, White (*Morus alba*). Spreading, round-topped tree with bright green leaves of diverse lobing. Small white fruits enjoyed by birds. Weeping mulberry is a dwarf variety, once popular. Height, 50 feet. Zone 4*.

Oak, Turkey (*Quercus cerris*). Broad head of many short branches. Narrow, unlobed leaf is dark green and glossy. A fine specimen tree. Height, 80 feet. Zone 6*.

Osage-orange (*Maclura pomifera*). Glossy dark green leaves. Distinctive fruit is green, furrowed, round, of 3-inch diameter; inedible. Thorny plant, once used for hedgerows in the Middle West. Height, 30 feet. Zone 6.

Paper-mulberry (*Broussonetia papyrifera*). Trunk often gnarled and picturesque. Will thrive under poor growing conditions. Suckers may be troublesome. Height, 35 feet. Zone 5*.

Paulownia, Royal (*Paulownia tomentosa*). Leaf and flower resemble catalpa, but flower is pale lavender, fragrant. Flower buds may be killed by cold weather. Height, 50 feet. Zone 6.

Pawpaw (*Asimina triloba*). Large leaves offer semi-tropical effect. Fruit has shape of a banana but flavor does not have the same appeal. Difficult to move; best grown from seed. Height, 30 feet. Zone 6.

Persimmon (*Diospyros virginiana*). Dark glossy leaf. Orange-colored fruit should not be eaten until after a frost mellows it. Height, 25 feet. Zone 5*.

Pine, Limber (*Pinus flexilis*). Evergreen becoming flat-topped at maturity. Slow growing; similar to white pine but smaller. Height, 30 feet. Zone 2.

Pine, Pitch (*Pinus rigida*). Evergreen of picturesque habit, but does not have the refinement of most pines. Will grow on poor soil. Height, 45 feet. Zone 5.

Pine, Red (*Pinus resinosa*). Dark green, moderately coarse evergreen. Will grow on poor soil. Insect and disease problems have become serious in recent years. Height, 60 feet. Zone 3.

Poplar, White (*Populus alba*). White fuzzy growth on lower side of leaf gives unusual appearance. Height, 70 feet. Zone 3*.

Redwood, Dawn (*Metasequoia glyptostroboides*). Non-evergreen conifer; foliage resembles hemlock. Fast growing. Was thought to be extinct until found in China in 1947. Height, 80 feet. Zone 5*.

Sassafras (*Sassafras albidum officinale*). Tall, straight trunk with short, horizontal side branches, the lower ones gradually dropping off. Leaves of variable shape are showy in autumn: yellow, orange-yellow, scarlet. Height, 60 feet. Zone 5.

Spruce, Serbian (*Picea omorika*). Evergreen. Makes an attractive specimen with dark green needles. Takes up less ground space than other spruces. Rare. Height, 60 feet. Zone 4*.

Sugarberry (*Celtis laevigata*). Broad, rounded head with branches often pendulous. Generally resistant to the witches'-broom that attacks other species of *Celtis*. Withstands drought and other poor growing conditions. Height, 80 feet. Zone 6.

Sycamore (*Platanus occidentalis*). Heavy frame with attractive light-colored, mottled bark. Leaf is affected by anthracnose disease in wet spring. Sometimes called Buttonball. Height, 90 feet. Zone 5.

Tree-of-Heaven (*Ailanthus altissima*). Compound leaf to 1½ feet long. Reddish seed pod on female plants. Tolerates poorest of growing conditions. Numerous seedlings and sprouts may prove to be troublesome. Height, 50 feet. Zone 5.

Yellowhorn (*Xanthoceras sorbifolium*). Flowers in clusters, up to 8 inches long; individual florets, 1 inch across, are white with carmine markings. Late May. Glossy foliage. Height, 20 feet. Zone 6.

CHAPTER 17

Reference Charts

Botanical names, hardiness zones, and descriptions of these plants are given in Chapter 15.

Seasonal Effects

ATTRACTIVE FLOWERS

Trees	Flowering Time	Color
Camellia	Winter–early spring	Red, pink, white
Catalpa, Western	Late June	White
Cherry, Amanogawa Flowering	Mid-May	Light pink
——, Columnar Sargent	Late April	Pink
——, Kwanzan Flowering	Mid-May	Bluish pink
——, Sargent	Late April	Pink
——, Weeping Japanese	Late April	Light pink
Cherry-laurel	Late May	White
Cornelian-cherry	Early April	Light yellow
Crab-apple, Flowering	Mid-May	Variable
——, Siberian	Early May	White
Crape-myrtle	Summer	Pink
Dogwood, Flowering	Mid-May	White
——, Japanese	June	White
——, Pink Flowering	Mid-May	Pink
Enkianthus, Redvein	Mid-May	Cream, red veins
Franklinia	September–October	White
Fringe-tree	Early June	White
Goldenchain, Waterer	Late May	Yellow
Goldenrain-tree	Mid-July	Yellow
Hardy-orange	Late April	White
Hawthorn, Cockspur	Late May	White
——, Paul's Scarlet	Late May	Pink
——, Washington	Mid-May	White
Lilac	Mid-May	Lilac, white
——, Japanese Tree	Mid-June	Creamy white
Magnolia, Hokkaido	Late April	White

Magnolia, Saucer	Early May	White
———, Southern	Late May	White
———, Star	Late April	White
———, Sweet-bay	Late May	White
Maple, Norway	Late April	Yellow-green
———, Red	Early April	Red
Mountain-ash, European	Late May	White
———, Korean	Late May	White
Mountain-laurel	Mid-June	White to pink
Nannyberry	Late May	White
Peach, Double White Flowering	Late April	White
Pear, Bradford	Early May	White
Pea-tree, Siberian	Mid-May	Yellow
Plum, Thundercloud	Late April	White to pink
Privet, Glossy	July	Creamy white
Quince, Chinese	Early May	Light pink
Redbud, Eastern	Mid-May	Magenta
———, White	Mid-May	White
Rhododendron, Rosebay	Early July	White
Rose-of-Sharon	August	Varied
Scholar-tree, Chinese	Early August	Cream
Shadblow, Allegheny	Late April	White
Silk-tree	July–September	White to pink
———, Hardy	July–September	Pink
Silverbell, Carolina	Mid-May	White
———, Mountain	Mid-May	White
Snowbell, Japanese	Early June	White
Sorrel-tree	Mid-July	White
Stewartia, Korean	July	White
Tulip-tree	Mid-June	Greenish yellow
Viburnum, Blackhaw	Mid-May	White
———, Siebold	Late May	White
Yellow-wood	Mid-June	White

TREES WITH SHOWY FRUITS

Buckthorn	Hawthorn, Washington
Cork-tree, Amur	Holly, American
Crab-apple, Flowering	———, Dahoon
Cucumber-tree	———, Yaupon
Dogwood, Flowering	Mountain-ash, European
———, Japanese	———, Korean
Goldenrain-tree	Privet, Glossy
Hardy-orange	Spindle-tree, European
Hawthorn, Cockspur	Viburnum, Siebold

TREES WITH BRIGHT AUTUMN FOLIAGE

Birch, Columnar White
————, Gray
————, Paper
Cherry, Columnar Sargent
————, Sargent
Dogwood, Flowering
————, Japanese
Enkianthus, Redvein
Franklinia
Ginkgo
Hawthorn, Cockspur
Honey-locust, Sunburst
————, Thornless
Hornbeam, European
Katsura
Maple, Bloodleaf Japanese
————, Japanese
————, Red

Maple, Sugar
————, Trident
Mountain-ash, Korean
Nannyberry
Oak, Pin
————, Red
————, Scarlet
————, Willow
Pear, Bradford
Pepperidge
Shadblow, Allegheny
Sorrel-tree
Stewartia, Korean
Sweet-gum
Tulip-tree
Viburnum, Blackhaw
Yellow-wood
Zelkova

TREES WITH COLORFUL BARK

Beech, American
————, European
Birch, Columnar White
————, Gray
————, Paper
Cork-tree, Amur
Crape-myrtle
Dogwood, Japanese
Enkianthus, Redvein
Goldenchain, Waterer
Holly, Dahoon

Holly, Yaupon
Hornbeam, European
Maple, Paperbark
Mountain-ash, Korean
Pine, Lace-bark
————, Scotch
Plane, London
Shadblow, Allegheny
Stewartia, Korean
Yellow-wood
Zelkova

Soil Conditions for Trees

TOLERANT TREES

The trees named here will adapt themselves to almost any situation. Good drainage is, however, required for all except those marked "PDS," which will grow satisfactorily in poorly drained soil.

Birch, Gray
Buckthorn

Catalpa, Western
Cherry, Kwanzan Flowering

Cork-tree, Amur
Crab-apple, Flowering, PDS
———, Siberian, PDS
Crape-myrtle
Douglas-fir
Elm, American, PDS
———, Camperdown
———, Chinese
———, Siberian
Fringe-tree
Ginkgo
Goldenrain-tree
Hardy-orange
Hawthorn, Cockspur
Holly, Dahoon, PDS
———, Japanese
———, Yaupon, PDS
Honey-locust, Thornless
Hornbeam, Hop
———, European
———, Pyramid European
Juniper, Blue Columnar Chinese
Lilac
———, Japanese Tree
Linden, Little-leaf
———, Silver
Magnolia, Hokkaido
Maple, Norway
———, Red, PDS
———, Scanlon, PDS
———, Silver, PDS
Mountain-ash, Korean
Nannyberry, PDS
Oak, Red
———, Scarlet
———, White

Oak, Willow, PDS
Peach, Double White Flowering
Pear, Bradford
Pea-tree, Siberian
Pepperidge, PDS
Pine, Austrian
———, Eastern White
———, Japanese Black
———, Lace-bark
———, Mugo
———, Scotch
———, Swiss Stone
Plane, London
Plum, Thundercloud
Poplar, Carolina
———, Japanese
———, Lombardy
Privet, Glossy
Quince, Chinese
Red-cedar
Rose-of-Sharon
Russian-olive
Scholar-tree, Chinese
Sea-buckthorn
Shadblow, Allegheny
Silverbell, Mountain
Spindle-tree, European
Spruce, Norway
Sweet-gum, PDS
Viburnum, Blackhaw
———, Siebold
Willow, Babylon Weeping, PDS
———, Contorted Hankow,
    PDS
Yew, Upright Japanese
Zelkova

TREES THAT REQUIRE FERTILE SOIL

Good drainage is also required for all listed here, except those marked "PDS," which will grow satisfactorily in poorly drained soil.

Arborvitae, American, PDS
———, Pyramidal, PDS

Beech, Copper
———, Dawyck

Beech, European
————, Weeping
Birch, Columnar White
————, Paper
Box, Tree
Camellia
Cedar, Blue Atlas
Cherry, Amanogawa Flowering
————, Columnar Sargent
————, Sargent
————, Weeping Japanese
Cherry-laurel
Cornelian-cherry
Cryptomeria
Cucumber-tree
Devilwood
Dogwood, Flowering
————, Japanese
————, Welch Flowering
Enkianthus, Redvein
Fir, White
Franklinia
Fringe-tree
Goldenchain, Waterer
Hawthorn, Paul's Scarlet
————, Washington
Hemlock, Canada
————, Carolina
————, Japanese
————, Sargent Weeping
Holly, American
Katsura

Magnolia, Saucer
————, Southern
————, Star
————, Sweet-bay, PDS
Maple, Bloodleaf Japanese
————, Columnar Sugar
————, Hedge
————, Japanese
————, Paperbark
————, Sugar
————, Trident
Mountain-ash, European
Mountain-laurel
Oak, Pin, PDS
————, Pyramidal English
————, Sawtooth
————, Shingle
Pine, Silver Japanese White
————, Tanyosho
Redbud, Eastern
Rhododendron, Rosebay, PDS
Silk-tree
Silverbell, Carolina
Smoke-tree, American
Snowbell, Japanese
Sorrel-tree
Spruce, Colorado
————, Colorado Blue
Stewartia, Korean
Tulip-tree
Umbrella-pine
Yellow-wood

Special Sites

SEASHORE

Cryptomeria
Holly, Yaupon
Pine, Japanese Black
————, Scotch
Plane, London
Privet, Glossy

Rose-of-Sharon
Russian-olive
Sea-buckthorn
Umbrella-pine
Yew, Upright Japanese
Zelkova

CITY GARDEN

Birch, Columnar White
Buckthorn
Cork-tree, Amur
Douglas-fir
Ginkgo
Goldenrain-tree
Hawthorn, Washington
Honey-locust, Shademaster
Linden, Little-leaf
———, Silver
Magnolia, Saucer
Maple, Erect Norway
———, Globe Norway

Maple, Hedge
———, Norway
Oak, Red
———, Sawtooth
Pine, Scotch
Plane, London
Privet, Glossy
Rose-of-Sharon
Scholar-tree, Chinese
Willow, Babylon Weeping
———, Contorted Hankow
Yew, Upright Japanese

STREET

Cork-tree, Amur
Crab-apple, Columnar Siberian
———, Hopa
———, Katherine
———, Siberian
Dogwood, Flowering
Elm, American
Ginkgo
Goldenrain-tree
Hawthorn, Paul's Scarlet
Honey-locust, Shademaster
Hornbeam, Hop
Lilac, Japanese Tree
Linden, Little-leaf
———, Silver
Magnolia, Hokkaido
———, Southern
Maple, Cleveland

Maple, Columnar Sugar
———, Erect Norway
———, Globe Norway
———, Hedge
———, Norway
———, Scanlon
Mountain-ash, Korean
Oak, Red
———, Sawtooth
———, Scarlet
———, Willow
Plane, London
Privet, Glossy
Scholar-tree, Chinese
Silverbell, Mountain
Smoke-tree, American
Sweet-gum
Zelkova

Bibliography

A FEW HELPFUL REFERENCE VOLUMES

Brooklyn Botanic Garden. *Flowering Trees* (1963); *Fruits in the Home Garden* (1961); *Gardening in Containers* (1958); *Pruning Handbook* (1958); *Where to Buy 1000 Trees and Shrubs for Special Uses* (1960). Brooklyn, New York.

Clark, Robert B. *Flowering Trees.* Princeton, New Jersey: D. Van Nostrand Company, Inc., 1963.

den Boer, Arie F. *Flowering Crabapples.* Washington, D.C.: American Association of Nurserymen, 1959.

Hamblin, Stephen F. *Lists of Plant Types for Landscape Planting.* Cambridge, Massachusetts: Harvard University Press, 1929.

International Shade Tree Conference. *Shade Tree Evalution.* (1965). 1827 Neil Avenue, Columbus, Ohio.

New Jersey Federation of Shade Tree Commissions. *Trees for New Jersey Streets.* New Brunswick, New Jersey: Rutgers College of Agriculture, 1961.

Perkins, Harold O. *Espaliers and Vines for the Home Gardener.* Princeton, New Jersey: D. Van Nostrand Company, Inc., 1964.

Pirone, Pascal P. *Tree Maintenance.* New York: Oxford University Press, 1959.

———, Bernard O. Dodge, Harold W. Rickett. *Diseases and Pests of Ornamental Plants.* New York: Ronald Press Company, 1960.

Reed, Clarence A., and John Davidson. *The Improved Nut Trees of North America.* New York: Devin-Adair Company, 1958.

Robinson, Florence Bell. *Useful Trees and Shrubs* (A card file). Champaign, Illinois: The Garrand Press, 1960.

Taloumis, George. *Outdoor Gardening in Pots and Boxes.* Princeton, New Jersey: D. Van Nostrand Company, Inc., 1962.

Taylor, Albert D. *The Complete Garden.* Garden City, New York: Doubleday, Page & Company, 1924.

United States Department of Agriculture. "Plant Hardiness Zone Map." Miscellaneous Publication No. 814 (1960). Superintendent of Documents, U.S. Government Printing Office, Washington, D.C.

Viertel, Arthur T. *Trees, Shrubs and Vines, A Pictorial Guide to the Ornamental Woody Plants of the Northeastern United States Exclusive of Conifers.* Syracuse, New York: College of Forestry, Syracuse University, 1959.

Wigginton, Brooks E. *Trees and Shrubs for the Southeast.* Athens, Georgia: University of Georgia Press, 1963.

Wyman, Donald. *Trees for American Gardens.* New York: The Macmillan Company, 1951.

Yoshimura, Yuri, and Giovanna M. Halford. *Japanese Art of Miniature Trees and Landscapes.* Rutland, Vermont: Charles E. Tuttle Company, 1960.

Index

The index includes only the botanical names of the trees. They are listed alphabetically according to common name in Part 3, "Descriptive Lists and Landscape Uses."

189